novum pro

Cléa Formaz
Photography by Manuela Sezer

HEART ON THE BRAIN

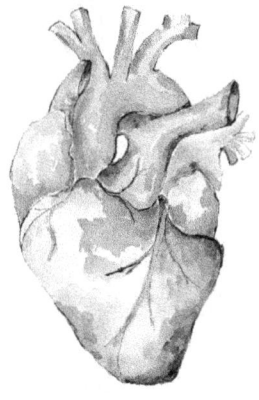

Heartbeats,
Decision-Making
and Human Identity

novum pro

www.novum-publishing.co.uk

All rights of distribution,
including via film, radio, and television,
photomechanical reproduction,
audio storage media, electronic data
storage media, and the reprinting of
portions of text, are reserved.

Printed in the European Union on
environmentally friendly, chlorine- and
acid-free paper.

© 2021 novum publishing

ISBN 978-3-99107-331-4
Editing: Ashleigh Brassfield, DipEdit
Cover photo: Manuela Sezer
Cover design, layout & typesetting:
novum publishing
Internal illustrations:
Photography by Manuela Sezer,
page 3: Cléa Formaz,
page 71–110, 41–42: Shutterstock

www.novum-publishing.co.uk

CONTENT

About the Book 9

Preface 15

1. Introduction 17
   The Human Heart 19
   The Human Brain 21
   Who are we, and what defines us? 26
   Work in progress 38
   What does it mean to be human? 42
   Existentialism – How free are we? 51
   Heart on the Brain 60

2. Know Your Own Heart 67
   The Anatomy of the Heart 69
   The Electrocardiogram 73
   Autonomic Nervous System 75
   Heart rate variability 77
   Heartbeat perception 80

3. Know Your Brain 89
   Plastic Brains 93
   Decision-Making 98

4. The Heart-Brain Interaction 105
   The Somatic Marker Hypothesis 111
   The Heart-Brain Coherence 113
   Understanding Our Consciousness 116

5. We feel, therefore we are 117

6. Enhancing Inner Awareness Through
   Mindfulness and Self-Perception 127

7. Listen to your heartbeat 133
   The heart on the brain:
   Are heartbeats part of our identity? 135

Acknowledgements 141

Endnotes 143

Thank you

For Love

*Sometimes my heart beats shallow,
and sometimes it beats so strong I think my chest will burst.*

*When I'm running, my heart beats fast. When I'm reading,
writing or having tea with grandma, it beats slow.*

*My heart beats for love. For the people I love,
for the profession I love, for a life I love.*

What else is a heart for?

For without love, why would we need a pump?

By Cléa Formaz

ABOUT THE BOOK

While trying to find a definition of who we are as humans might take us on an inner journey to self-knowledge, we can see the correlation of the human heart and the human brain as an essential part in developing our ability to make conscious decisions throughout our lives.

Who are we? What defines us?

So many aspects should be taken into consideration when questioning who we are and what defines us. What makes us distinctive as individuals? If looking into the core of human existence, we are all the same. However, while paving our path through our human journey, our individual experiences and emotions make us unique as a person.

It is important to know your own heart, not only as of the biological pump that provides cells with oxygen and nutrients but also as the core of feelings and emotions. Also, understand how your brain is liable for building your identity as an individual since it is responsible for the decision-making. The brain's ability to make decisions is directly connected to choosing who we are and who we will become.

But how do we make decisions? How does the brain make decisions?

When the heart and brain interact, the heart continually sends signals to the brain, giving rise to how we feel. The heart and the mind seem to be working in unison, constant communication and interaction.

Feelings and emotions, like joy or sorrow, are responsible for influencing the dynamics of the heart. Since the brain is connected to the heart, once it has received this "information," the brain's decision-making process is based on this interaction and experience.

As humans, when we have experiences in life capable of modifying our heartbeats, this interaction is responsible for influencing the brain process and changing the result, including decision-making. The perception of our own heartbeats has been shown to influence behaviour as well. When an experience is too scary or exciting, our decisions may differ based on emotions and feelings.

Learning to look into the core of ourselves, as humans, and listen to our own heartbeats will help us evolve as humans.

The question "can the heart think and feel?" will always be an example to be explored in human existence. If the brain is an essential part of creating our identity, can we consider the heart to play a crucial role as well?

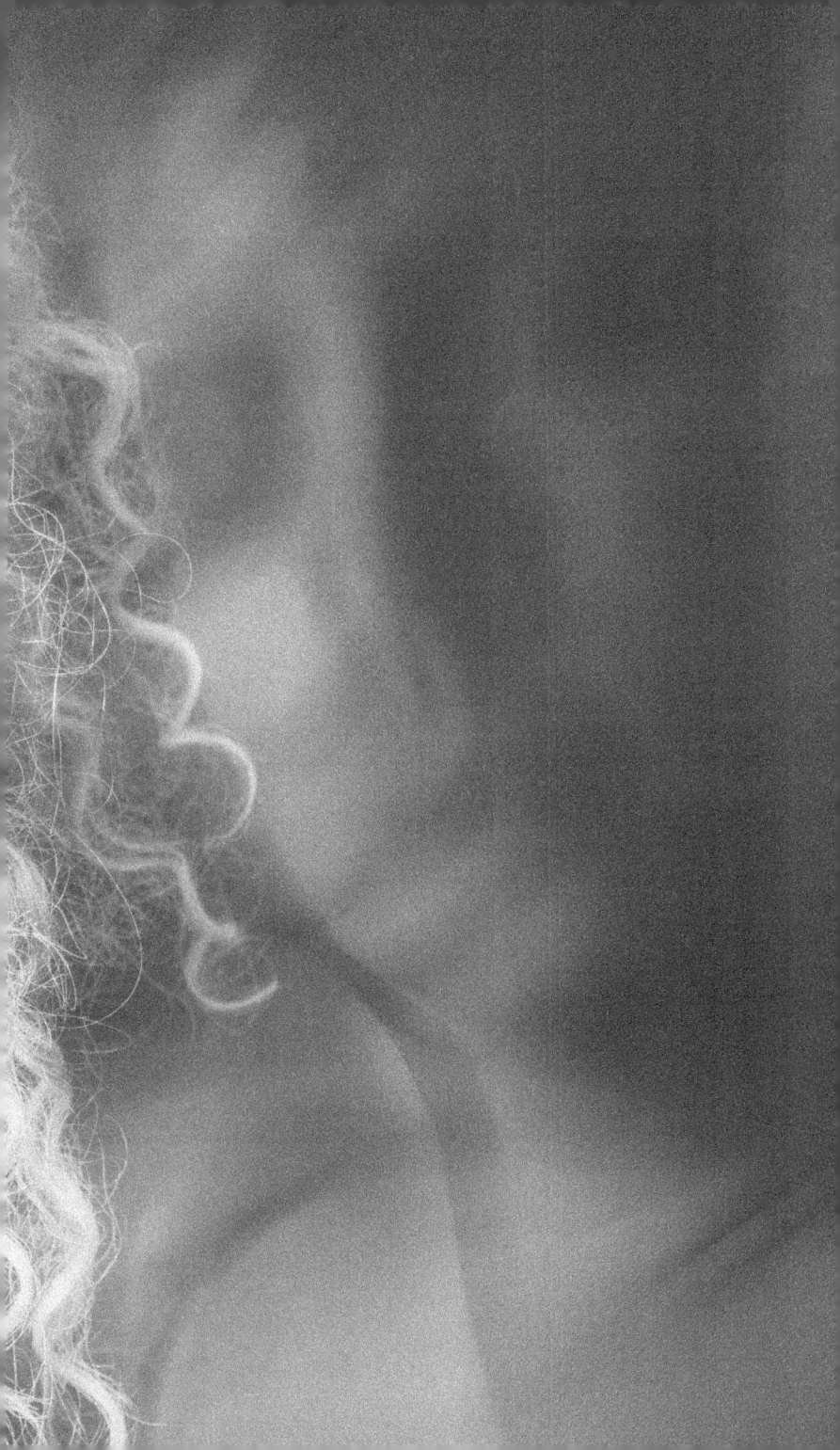

PREFACE

We often define ourselves based on a specific characteristic, passion, or job. When times get tough, we feel as though our whole identity has been stripped away. By building a rich identity that encompasses the many facets of your personality, you can weather any storm without losing yourself in the process. With this book, I encourage you to look at the many aspects that may be part of who you are.

With this book, I also intend to provide a new perspective on human identity through the heart. Too often, we rely on our brain to tell us who we are. Turn a listening ear inward to discover the richness of the heart-brain interaction and truly understand yourself.

I would also like to challenge you to think about the concrete truths you hold about the world and yourself, and come up with your own interpretations, views, and perspectives that stem from within.

To know the depths of your heart and your brain is to truly know yourself.

Knowing yourself is the basis of finding your purpose and discovering your passion. Discovering your passion will unlock the door to a fulfilled life by leading you towards what's important… and away from what isn't.

1. INTRODUCTION

Humans, like all living creatures, are intrinsically complex and sentient beings. Our physical bodies are extraordinarily complicated, and every organ has a crucial role to play. However, the heart and the brain more frequently come up in conversations about biology, science, consciousness, spirituality, and religion than any other part of the human body. For centuries, the interaction between the heart and brain has been a source of intrigue and wonder.

Emotionally, scientifically, and philosophically, the relationship between the heart and brain has been explored in order to answer the great existential questions of the human condition, not only biologically, in the way they sustain life and keep us healthy, but also how they influence our emotions, thoughts, perception of the self and the choices we make and the mechanisms driving them.

Without one or the other, we are incomplete – and the same can be said for each one of us as individuals. Within life, we each have a special purpose that is unique only to us, and our presence is an integral part of the society and universe in which we exist.

The Human Heart

Centuries ago, when scientists were just beginning to research the workings of the human body, they focused on the heart as the physical centre of not only our life but our intelligence and emotions as well. However, with scientific developments, they realized that the heart is not a chamber for our souls but is instead a biological pump. This does not reduce its significance. Our hearts pump life-giving oxygen and nutrients throughout our body, feeding our other organs and ensuring that everything is working perfectly and in unison.

The association between the heart and human emotions run deep in the human psyche to this day. When we are frightened, we feel our heart beating hard as our blood pressure rises. In sadness, we experience heartache as our muscles tighten and constrict. Someone in love may feel a fluttering sensation as their pulse rate quickens. It turns out that these are so much more than metaphors. Instead, a part of the fascinating way we experience feelings, physically as well as psychologically.

Indeed, there is a phenomenon known as the 'heart-brain', referring to the fact that the cardiac nervous system of our heart is an intricate system consisting of 40,000 neurons, which are very similar to the neurons found in the brain. There is no doubt that referring to the heart as only a biological pump is selling it short. Science has revealed that, as an intelligent organ, it engages in constant communication with the brain.

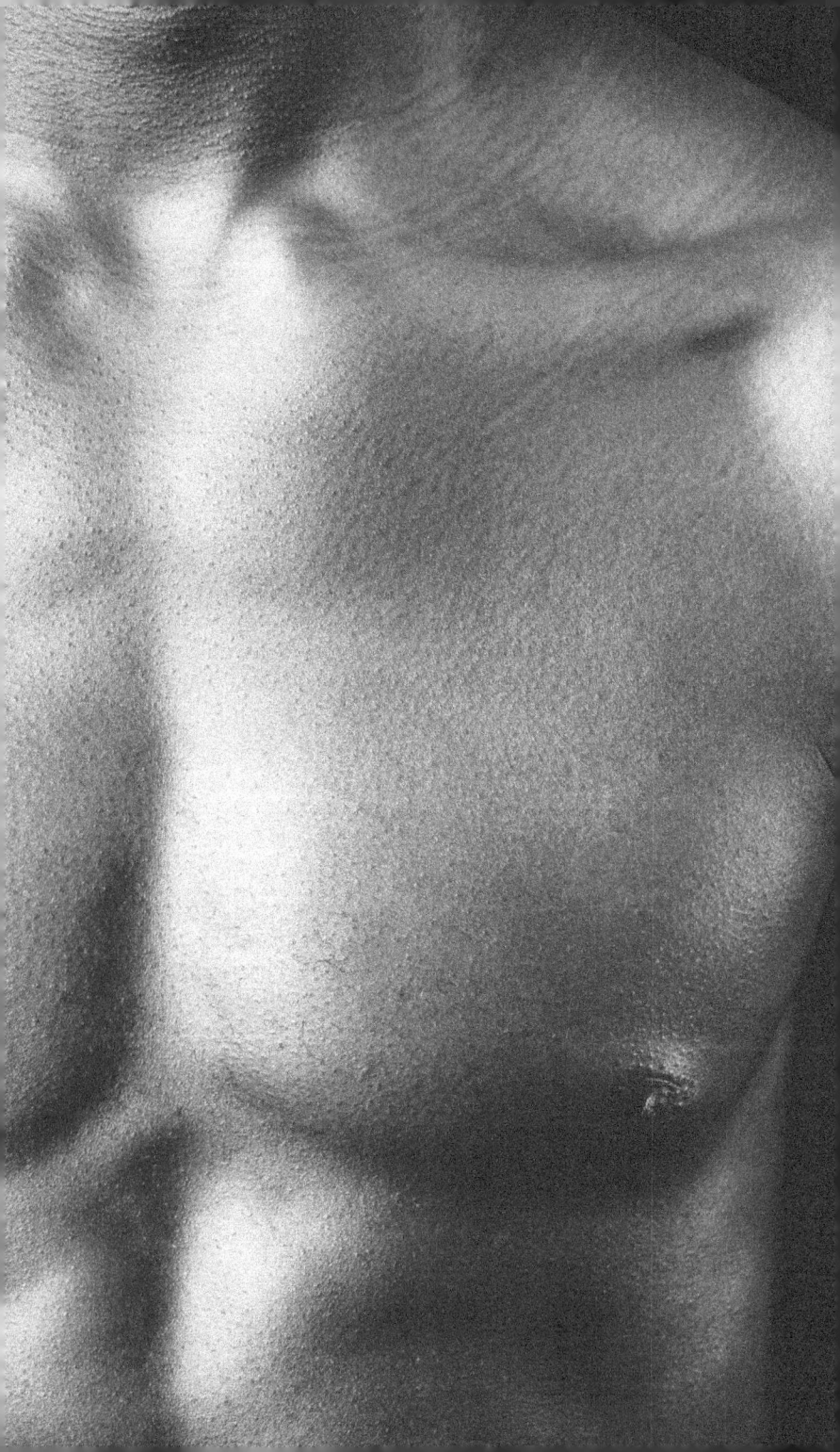

The Human Brain

The heart evidently has a role to play in our experiences, emotions, and actions. However, focusing only on the heart, at the expense of the brain, would restrict us from truly understanding our human consciousness. Our experiences, interpretations, beliefs, values, and subsequent attitudes, decisions, and choices, all arise from the mental processes happening in our brains.

As the command centre for the nervous system, the brain receives signals as electronic impulses from the body's sensory organs and then relays the information to the muscles. Essentially, human consciousness would be impossible without the brain. Composed of billions of nerve cells, countless nerve fibres and literally trillions of connections, the brain is the driving centre for our perceptions of the world, the ways in which we interpret our experiences, our memories, our sense of self and identity, and the choices we make and their resulting actions.

This highly sophisticated and specialised organ regulates every major and minor system within our bodies. It not only directs our bodies' internal functions but integrates sensory impulses from the outside world and the information coming from our internal thoughts and observations. Whilst it weighs only three pounds, the brain is the source of our entire consciousness and – by extension – what it is to be human.

While the functioning of the brain might be complex, I live by the philosophy of explanatory parsimony: Even humanity's most difficult discoveries can be explained in simple English. In other words, in order for our work to become helpful to society, we should be able to explain it simply.

I live by this philosophy myself; though, of course, I risk losing some of the nuances of the inherently complex issues under discussion. The subjects I will be discussing here, the heart and brain, are inherently complex. In this book, I am not aiming to spend too much time analysing these individual parts but hope to scratch on the correlation of the two. While I cannot promise to capture the whole scientific picture, I do hope to begin a questioning process, which then addresses fundamental questions that have likely been nagging at you. I begin by tackling the biggest philosophical question of all: Who are we?

Who are we, and what defines us?

Coming from a small town in the French part of Switzerland, surrounded by mountains and a stunning landscape, I soon understood that nothing should be taken for granted. At an early age, I was told that my mother's pregnancy was not planned; however, in a conscious decision, my parents agreed not to end the pregnancy. It was my first lesson in life: be grateful to favourable circumstances.

While growing up, I was taught many lessons about life. Those lessons were predefined by a mix of occurrences surrounding me, like my origins, my parent's backgrounds, societal expectations, religion, gender, and the environment I was in.

Once I started to mature and had more understanding about my surroundings and having my own experiences in life, I realised that I am more than those predefined concepts given to me while growing up. I realised I could not fit in the predesignated "box" I was put in.

The more rural nature of the country taught me to get used to the quiet. Life can get quite hectic, but during these lonely evening hours, I figured out what my thoughts were on certain things. When I was away from home, it was during these quiet evening hours in solitude that made me realise that we cannot be solely reduced to our origins or to a predefinition. That would reduce ourselves to homesickness and a limited aspect.

As a young teenager, I discovered athletics and all the dynamics of emotions and feelings my heart presented to me. I then learned how important all those complex feelings were and how it could make me feel good or bad, and how essential it is to "feel" all the physical and mental changes in my body. All those emotions were moulding me into the person I would become.

As an athlete, I have faced many ups and downs; in times where I was not able to compete for many different reasons, it was almost like my identity was taken away from me. I had learned how introspection could be a gift, helping me to become mentally healthy, even when I was physically ill.

I also became aware that it can happen the other way around. Why are we mentally exhausted while our heart feels heavy, and why are we mentally strong when our heart feels in harmony? Have you ever asked yourself these questions? When life is close to the heart, we experience many ups and downs, and this is when we have to enjoy the ride and disregard what causes our feelings not to connect with our bodies.

As a teenager, I had spent most of my free time competing as a middle-distance athlete. Being in sports was not about toning my body; it was how I learned to connect and accept my tall and thin anatomy. It made me competitive, self-aware about my physique and how I should accept my anatomical structure.

In the early days, I was always in sports stadiums for practice and did not take long to learn about the word "sexy" and how it plays a different role in teens' lives, especially when the body shame and idea of "perfect look" come around. It did not feel right to me.

When someone does not accept their own body or is not happy with the way they look in the mirror, it makes them feel disconnected. The body and heart are at different frequencies. Judging someone because of their body structure, weight, height, and overall appearance is, by all means, wrong and does not define who the person is.

I took specific comments too seriously at times. I do not condone critiques; however, it took a heavy load on my feelings. With more time and life experience, I learned the true meaning of the word sensuality and boosted my confidence. Through sensuality, I discovered new aspects of life, love and the law of attraction. I learned that I am not defined by how I look; it is just a fraction of who I am.

The more I matured, the more I questioned myself about life and our existence. Who am I? And how will my story end? The last time I asked myself these sorts of questions was during a vacation at the Côte d'Azur. I was sitting by the beach in Villefranche-sur-Mer; the sun was slowly setting, but I was wide awake.

One of the more crucial lessons in my life was not taught at school, nor by anyone around. In fact, exploring the world was one of the many ways I learned to question myself and question the world around me. I became aware of my own weakness and strengths.

I became aware of what is really meaningful to me. I realised that even when I am in fancy and desired places, I feel the most comfortable at home, surrounded by lakes and mountains. That is where I feel complete.

Some of the most outstanding philosophers claim that you will never get anywhere until you ask yourself these sorts of questions. The French literature and the French élégance taught me a lot about human existence. Classics like *Madame Bovary* by Gustave Flaubert (1856), portraying the beautiful and charming Emma Bovary, who sees the world through a veil of romantic novels and fanciful sensibilities, and is constantly at odds with her marriage to the well-meaning Charles Bovary. Emma Bovary's constant search for beauty and luxury leads her into debt and ruin, and she struggled to separate her romanticised ideals with the reality of country life.

Madame Bovary taught me to search for meaningful work, for sense in life, for love. It taught me that if you first aim to discover true passion, give your best and help others, luxury will follow. I also learned that I tend to choose simplicity and elegance over fanciness. The more I learned, the more I questioned.

Do my genes define me? Or maybe my passions in life? Is a partner a big part of who I am now? Am I defined by the way I love or have experienced love? Is having children (or not) part of a person?

When many questions still tormented my mind, I decided to get a science degree and conduct research to address discussions about the core aspect of what it means to be human and how the heart and brain are interconnected.

You may call me a dreamer, but deep down, I believe that every human being is here for a reason and should question their existence in the core. We all should look at our surroundings and examine the aspects of our lives that might not make sense anymore, or maybe not bring the happiness we all deserve to feel in life.

I firmly believe that our experiences in life are singular and influence how we feel in different situations presented to us. However, I also understand that we are free to choose our path, make our own mistakes and learn our own lessons.

When aiming for a new position or choosing a partner for life, for example, we bring our past experiences and expectations to that new partnership. When we discover ourselves first, knowing our individual needs and desires in life, we bring the expectations to that new relationship.

Looking around, being aware of our surroundings and feeling the ambience we are evolving in will help us understand what makes us who we are today and what we want to become in the future. Starting from where you are at this very moment, you choose who you will be.

This might sound a bit unnerving, and maybe it is. Jean-Paul Sartre, one of the most popular French philosophers from the 20th century, always had the idea that the need to keep making decisions brings constant anxiety. He even heightened this anxiety by pointing out that what you do really matters.

That you should make your choices as though you were choosing on behalf of the whole of humanity, taking the entire burden of responsibility for how the human race behaves. Those are part of the reasons why making thoughtful decisions will bring you to where you want to be.

Have you ever asked yourself, "Who are you?"

You may be aware of where you came from, your origins and the environment when growing up, or the preconceived expectations about your life that were "given" to you when you were born. However, have you ever taken a moment to think about your heart and brain and how connected they are while posing yourself questions about your own existence, like "who am I?" What about your work life? Have you found the so-called work-life balance you always desired? How about your dream job? What motivates you every day? What brings you joy? Or the opposite; what makes you feel uncomfortable or unsettled?

Raising all these questions is an essential part of knowing who you are. You may not realise it, but every time you think about these events in your life, your heart may send signals of feeling to your brain – they are called emotion.

When we realise how our emotions and actions affect our feelings and how our human existence is more than just what we think, we understand the meaning of life.

Maybe you work to live, or maybe you work to save money or to provide a good life for your family. Maybe you're in love, maybe you're single. You may be attracted to women, men, or both sexes, and define yourself by the choice of your partner (or your partner's sex).

Maybe you love your profession, or activities you do in your free time and you include them in your attempt to define yourself. At some point, you might have also been wondering whether you can define yourself with your physical make-up; in other words, your body type, and the way you look in general.

Or you might have experienced certain situations where you received signals from your body, like euphoria, pain, or heartache, that changed you as a person. Then – maybe with a full or an empty heart – you might have analysed your mental state, your brain – and wondered whether you are the wiring of your brain.

All of this raises the question of Being and what it is for a thing to be. What does it mean to say that you, yourself, are? According to philosopher and phenomenologist Martin Heidegger, it is essential to ask yourself these sorts of questions. He added that, in confusing situations, it is suggested to apply the phenomenological method: disregard intellectual clutter, pay attention to things, and let them reveal themselves to you.

At once, boxed in by borders and yet transcendent and exhilarating. This is what we call human existence. Individual and concrete; colourful and dark; thrown into a world of beautiful diversity, where we are whatever we choose to make of ourselves. Responsible for everything we do, with certain limitations. But despite these limitations, we can choose to be passionately involved in personal projects of all kinds.

Quite ambiguous: I once thought borders boxed me in, and it must be either dark or colourful, but by addressing questions including what it really means to be human with all of its freedom and limitations, we can try to describe our experiences in a way that awakens us to ways of living more authentic lives. And by living more authentically, we may realise that we freely choose to box ourselves into personal passion projects.

We are a work in progress and always will be. That's why we should always chase happiness and be the best version of ourselves.

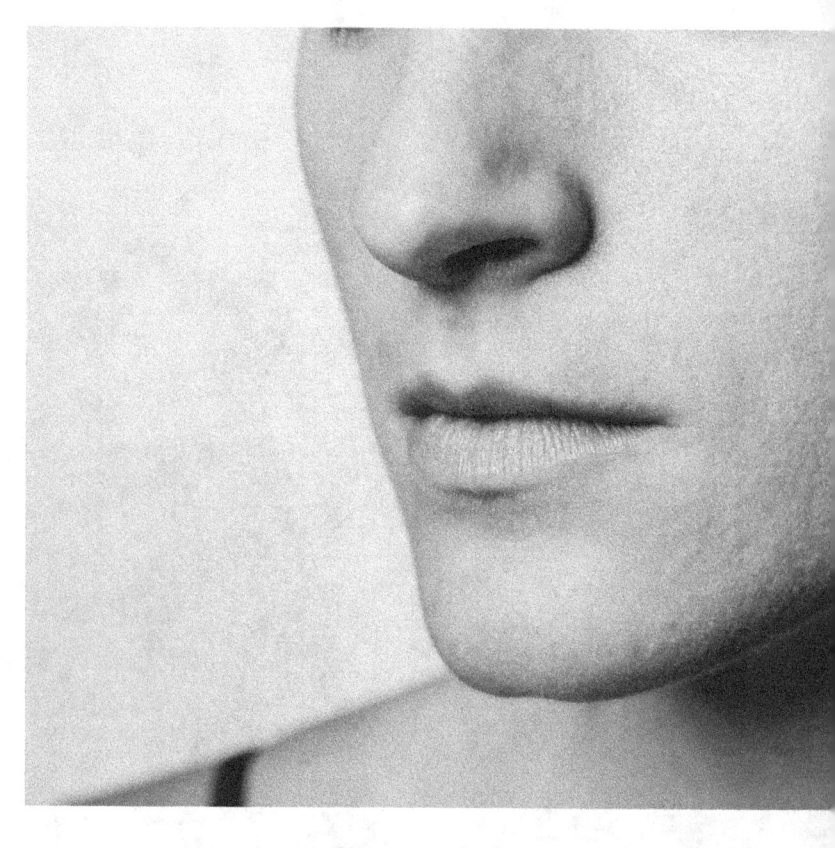

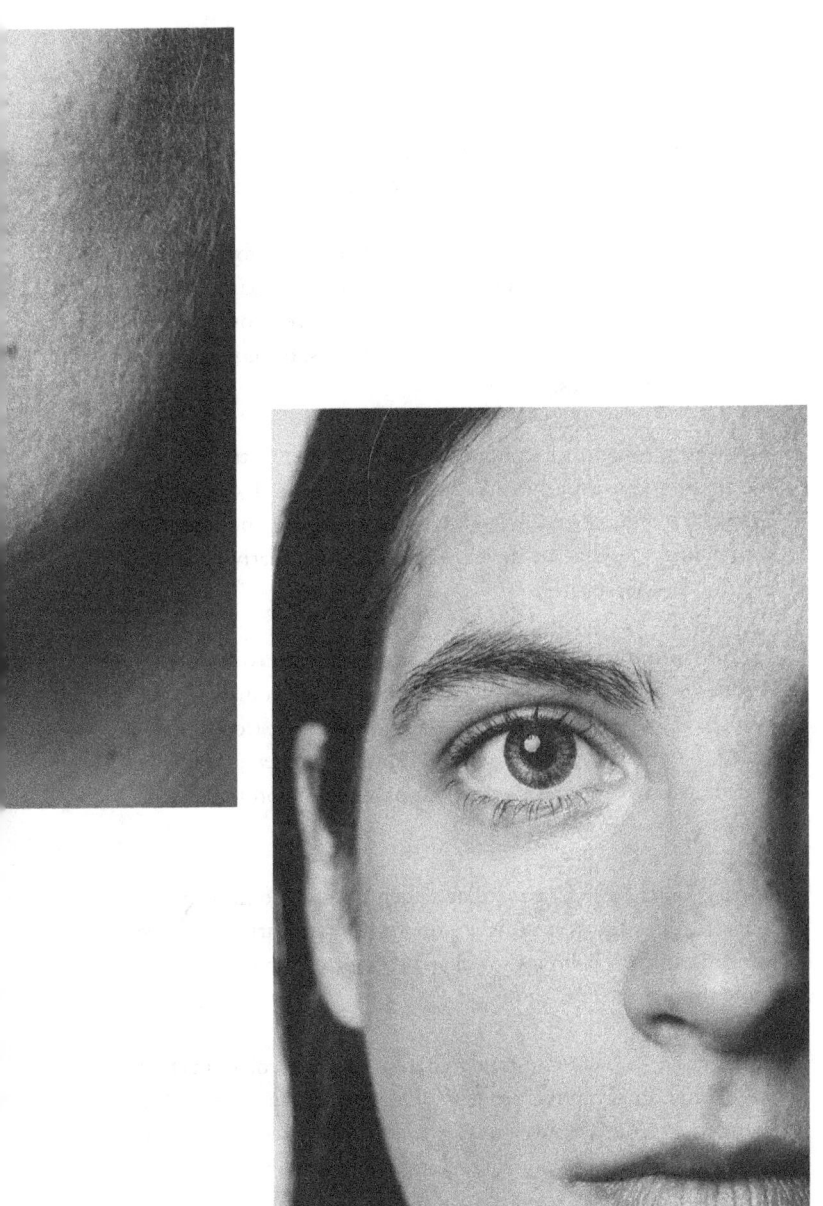

Work in progress

From growing up as a child, to adulthood, most of us are confronted with changes – and with that comes a reinvention.

You may fall in love, and you may decide to strive for a certain profession, putting everything you have into accomplishing your dream. These are all parts of the path you have chosen to follow. It may have taken you to different places, bringing with it different experiences.

The path is sometimes straight; at other times, it is strewn with the rocks and gravel that accumulate over time. Experiences shape us: they can knock us down, lift us up, or one after the other. They say that we develop strength and creativity out of failures and heartaches.

From a quite young age, we can choose a path to follow. A dream. A passion we discovered while we were young. Maybe you always wanted to become a doctor, manager, florist, hairstylist, or street clown. Or perhaps it just so happened that you ended up as a painter. Anyways, our passions and professions are a big part of who we are.

Events like choosing a particular career, passion, committing to a relationship, and becoming a mum or dad, are part of who we are and can change how we feel and see ourselves within a very short amount of time.

So, you see, you are constantly changing. The problem is that we mainly observe these aspects from an outer perspective. We mainly focus on what we see. We cannot really see our organs; therefore, we tend to not care enough about them.

But what if they are part of what we are and, most importantly, shape who we become? What if I tell you now that it is your heart and your brain that form the very basis of who you are? And that, by knowing them, you can choose more wisely the path in front of you to become the person you want to be?

Having a look at a philosophical perspective, French philosopher René Descartes' *Cogito, ergo sum*, (Latin for "I think, therefore I am) in his Discourse on Method (1637) is a first step in demonstrating the attainability of certain knowledge.

Descartes argued that even if an all-powerful demon were to try to deceive him into thinking that he exists when he does not, he would have to exist in order for the demon to deceive him. Therefore, whenever he thinks, he exists.

Furthermore, he argued that the statement "I am" (*sum*) expresses an immediate intuition, not the conclusion of a piece of reasoning (regarding the steps of which he could be deceived) and is thus indubitable.

However, in a later work, Principles of Philosophy (1644), Descartes suggested that the *cogito* is the conclusion of a syllogism whose premises include the propositions that he is thinking and whatever thinks must exist. This is the so-called dualist separation of mind and body from the 17th century.

While this theory surprisingly survived, it has been the target of much criticism. In *Descartes' Error: Emotion, Reason, and the Human Brain* in 1994, neurologist António Damásio presents the "somatic marker hypothesis." A proposed mechanism by which emotions guide (or bias) behaviour and decision-making, positing that rationality requires emotional input. He argues that René Descartes' "error" was the dualist separation of mind and body, rationality and emotion; that the mind and body, rather than separate, are interconnected.

By reading this book, you will learn about the recent discoveries of this connection and how it shapes you and your decisions and has consequences for your future.

It is important to find what you are passionate about; however, we should also start to turn the focus inward, to our heart and our brain, questioning why we have become the person we are. In this book, I will explain why.

I will explain why it is so important to find what makes your heartbeat and your brain respond, and why you should create your own definition of yourself.

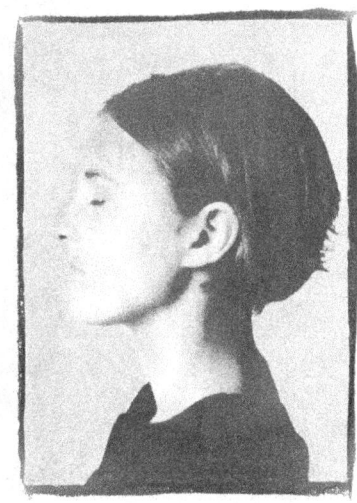

Ikonenbilder by Oliver Look

What does it mean to be human?

The definition of being human is as broad as our existence. It is not defined by one word or one simple occurrence in life. In fact, being human is constant change through the events and circumstances that happen in life.

Humans are born with some expectations in life, preconceived notions that are given at birth; how you should live, what you should believe, or who you should become. All those preconceived ideas are "boxed" and gifted to us.

Although our origins and even genes can be a large part of who we are, what will really define us as humans are the collective experiences in life that will build our identities for the future. When a person becomes aware of their surroundings and how life experiences are essential to moulding their future, questions begin to arise. With them, the ability to change the way we see the future and change ourselves.

"Who are we going to love?" and "what do we love?" are questions that will arise at some point in our human journey. Countless questions pave the path to finding a more meaningful life and understanding who we are.

Humans are free to make their own decisions in life, good or bad. How a person will make that decision and what that person expects the results to be, is based on personal experiences. How a person understands "action and reaction" is defined by previous experiences in life.

One undefined concept in human existence is how the heart and brain are connected, not only by biology but also in the complete sense of how it can mould our ability to make decisions based on emotions or logic.

The heart is often understood as a biological pump that provides our bodies with oxygen and nutrients. Although that is partially true, our heart is more than that. The heart sends signals of emotion to the brain that can affect our behaviours and decisions. These signals are part of this interaction between the mind and the heart. It is what gives us our identity.

All those factors are responsible for defining us as humans. Also, the way we interact as a collective group is accountable for defining us as individuals and society.

Scientifically, there is no right or wrong answer to who we are as humans. There are many factors to consider, and if we go to the core, the heart and the brain, these organs are too complex to understand fully. We can all raise the question of who we are, as an individual and also as a society.

We get closer to the core of our own existence by being aware of our surroundings and how they affect our lives—also understanding how we interact with others and how our emotions are affected by events.

Being aware of our own strengths and weaknesses is one of the first steps to understanding who we are as humans and what we want to become in the future. It is an essential part of understanding our existence and what we are as individuals.

Understanding our passions, desires, and uniqueness will help us better understand our purpose in life to understand our journey as humans and will help us to make wiser decisions to fill our days with happiness and love.

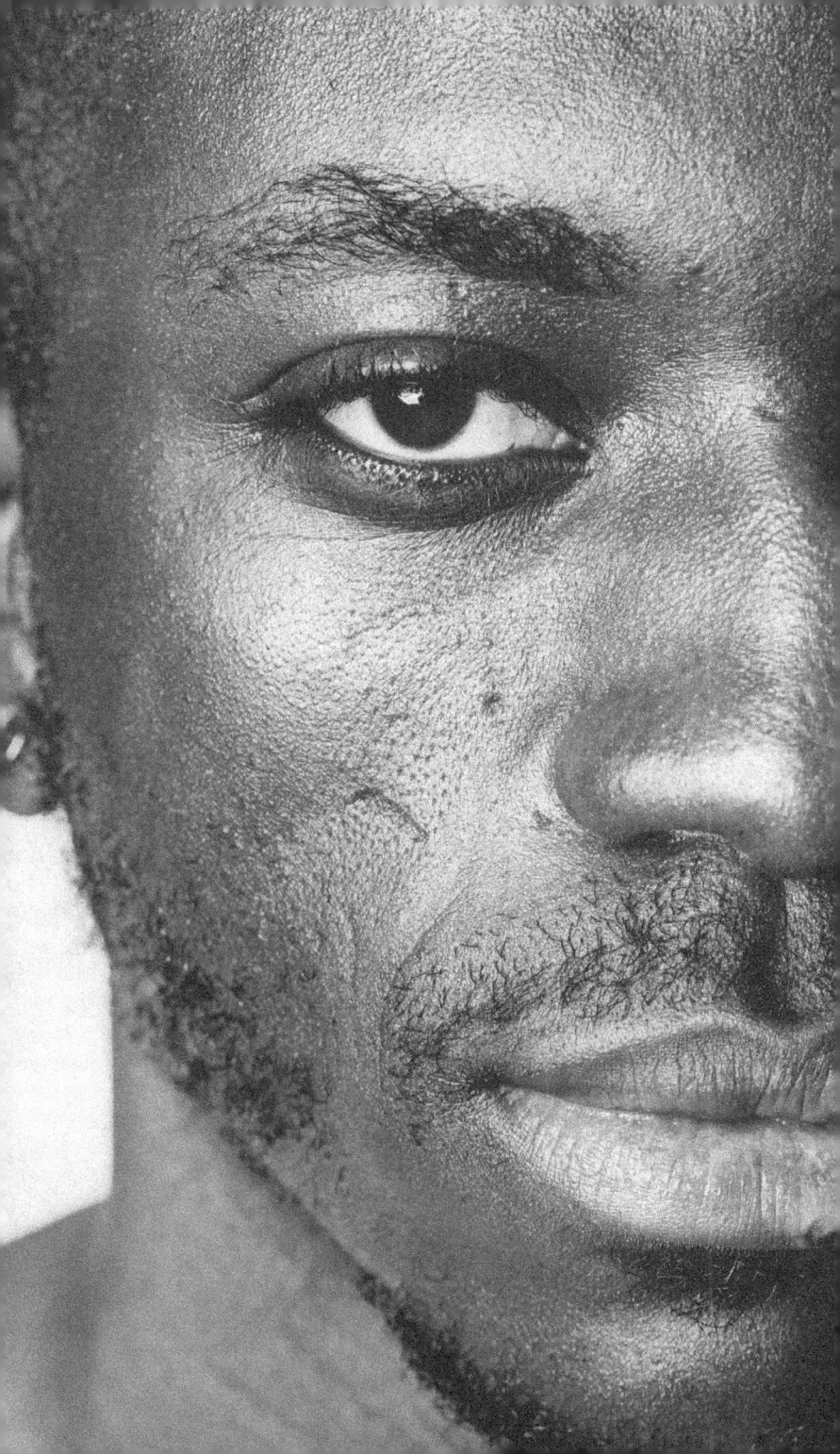

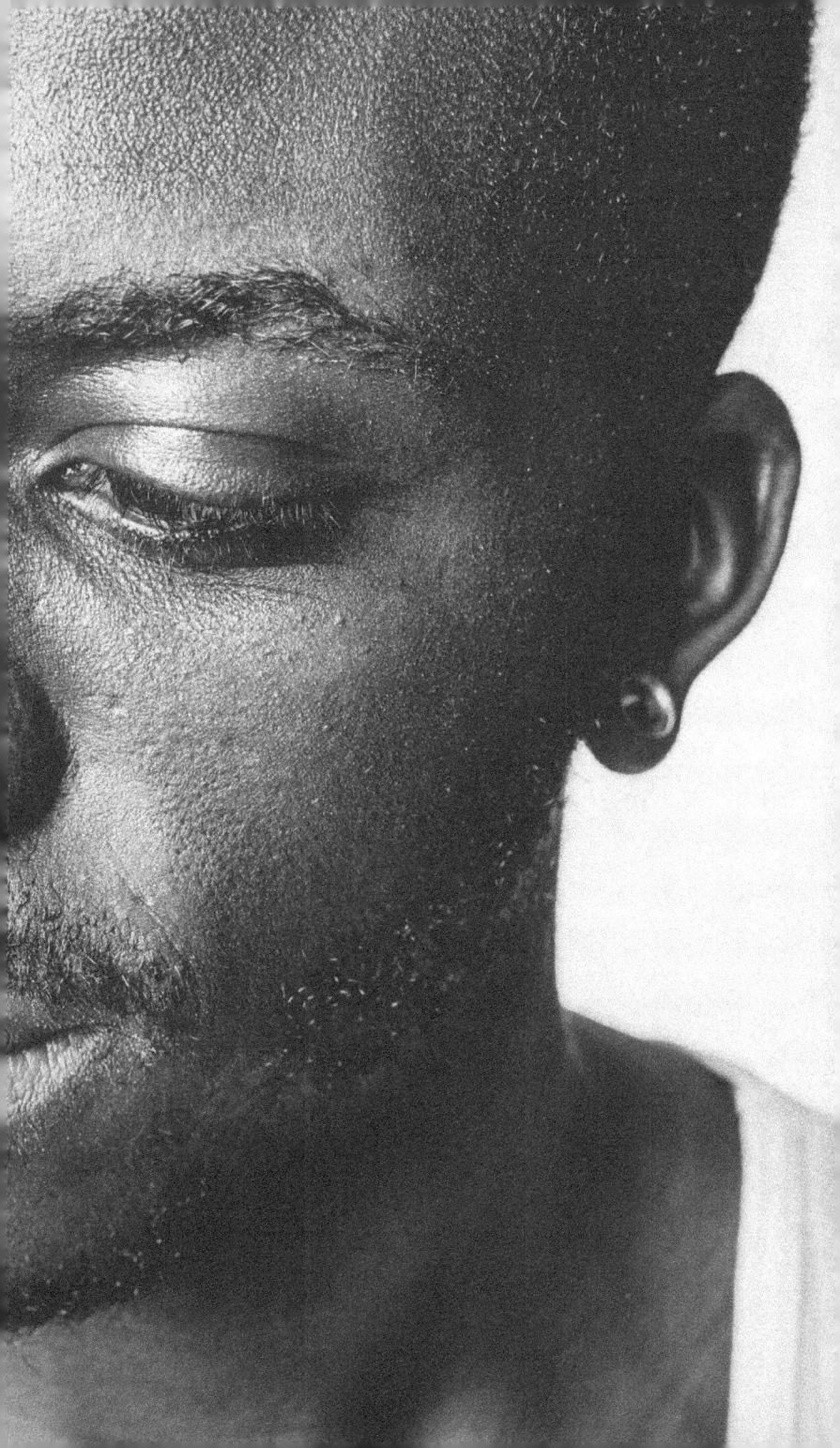

Existentialism – How free are we?

While contextualizing freedom is not so simple, the general idea can be simply explained as an action not constrained by the present state. Freedom can be implied in many areas of our lives, such as freedom of belief, speech, movement, choice, and individual expression.

After all, the definition of freedom can differ between various philosophers' and viewers' beliefs freedom applies to their own lives. However, one simple question can identify how you, as an individual, understand freedom, its implications to your own life and how it fits in society.

What does freedom mean to you? How free are you?

Jean-Paul Sartre wrote about the physical sensations of the world and the structures and moods of human life. Above all, he conveyed his idea about what it meant to be free. According to Sartre's philosophy, "freedom is the heart of all human experiences." For Sartre, existence precedes essence, freedom is unlimited and infinite, and existence is freedom.

Believing in free will and self-determination, Sartre's idea of freedom is that we do not have any predefined nature at all as a human being. Instead, we create that nature through what we choose to do. According to his philosophy, freedom may be influenced by biological, cultural, or individual backgrounds; however, it does not define us. We are free to make our own choices and choose our path throughout our existence.

Simone de Beauvoir, or the midwife of Sartre, as she used to call herself, claims that "to be free is not to have the power to do anything you like; it is to be able to surpass the given towards an open future; the existence of others as freedom defines my situation and is even the condition of my own freedom."

The central point of existentialism, "Existence precedes essence," understands that we are one step ahead of ourselves, choosing a path to go down, making ourselves up as we go along. It implies that we are not defined by labels or preconceived ideas about our existence. Instead, we create ourselves frequently through the actions taken and decisions made throughout our lives.

Sartre was vehement that we are our own freedom, no more and no less than that. We continuously create ourselves and will always be a work in progress.

When we confront ourselves, away from our comfort zones, we can confront our deepest fears and anxieties. That is when we can find our true essence, amidst the outside interferences we face every day.

As Sartre's biggest dilemma arose in the mid-1940s, he was looking for answers while still believing in the essence of existentialism, such as the empirical question: if we are free, how can we use our freedom well in challenging times?

Sartre claimed that it is always our choice and that nothing could stop us but our own free will. If we want to survive, we have to decide to live. Nothing can stop you. You are free to choose, but also to take responsibility for your choices.

The existential horror philosophy emphasises the uniqueness and isolation of the individual experience in a hostile or uninvolved world. It characterises the human existence as unexplainable and stresses the freedom of choice and responsibility as consequences of the individual's actions.

But with freedom of choice comes responsibility and doubt. The doubts triggered by exercising our freedom of choice are primarily linked to the uncertainties of our fundamental being. The world is fast enough to declare that we are out of control, with the numerous amounts of articles, theories, and science books proving nothing but a mere illusion of a conscious, governing mind. It primarily states that when we decide to sit down and reach for a glass of water, we are not really choosing at all. Instead, we are responding to tendencies and associations beyond the reach of both reason and will.

As advocated by Søren Kierkegaard and Albert Camus, the life of the absurd rejects any meaning to human existence, thus encouraging people to be themselves and do what makes them alive. Practically it is explained that any person who desires to exercise their freedom must accept to live the life of absurdity. Absurdity holds that there is no meaning to life except the one we give it.

> "The only way to deal with an unfree world is to become so absolutely free that your very existence is an act of rebellion."
> Albert Camus

Throughout your authentic existence, you are able to determine your freedom of being. Also, being free means not comparing ourselves to others. An authentic life means that as humans, we ought to be answerable to ourselves only; it is to be influenced by an individual's actions.

When practicing your authenticity, you can recognize that everyone is different in their journeys, ways of living, timing, and space needed to acquire the same goal. We are just different individuals in general.

Expectations also can limit our freedom of existence. When trying to be loved by others in what we consider the "right" way and not in the way others can give us love, as individuals, we create a deep resentment of our identity.

At once boxed in by borders and yet transcendent and exhilarating; this is what we call human existence. Individual and concrete. Colourful and dark. Thrown into a world of beautiful diversity, where we are whatever we choose to make of ourselves, responsible for everything we do – with certain limitations. But despite these limitations, we are free to choose our own paths.

This philosophy also acknowledges that if we have lost touch with our bodies, we may be listening to our insides in the wrong way. All the sensations and feelings we may have been experiencing are not easily identified. Feelings and sensations like uncertainty, anxiety, fears, and mental disturbances.

> "If a man has his eyes bound, you can encourage him as much as you like to stare through the bandage, but he'll never see anything."
> Franz Kafka, The Castle

When facing our inner world and recognising our emotions, perceptions, expectations, and reflections, we can better understand how our hearts and brains are interconnected. Each of these, along with science and philosophy, is one piece of the whole. We should turn ourselves inward and listen to the depth of our emotions and feelings to better understand our human existence as individuals. We start by getting to know the heart and the brain.

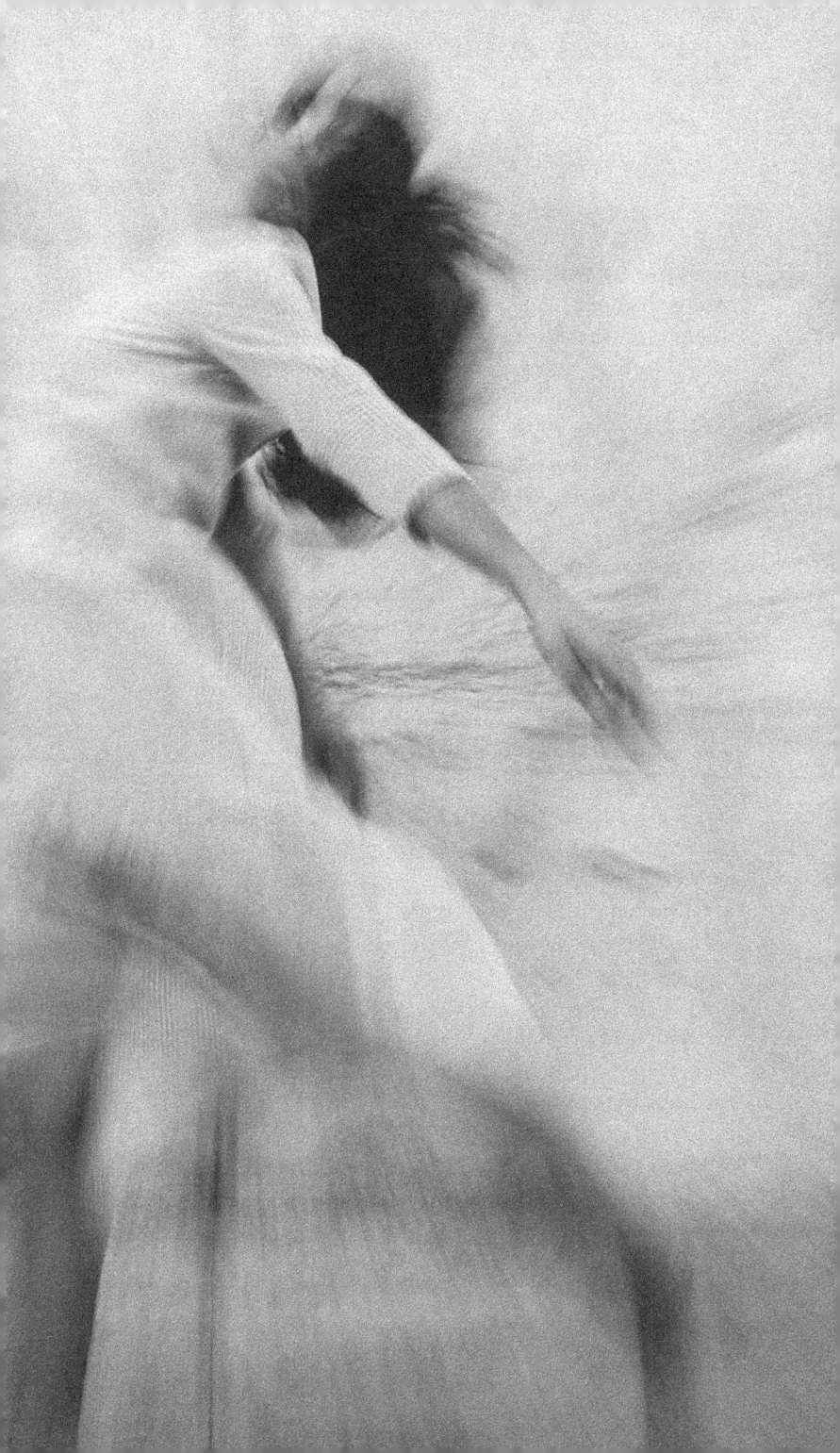

Heart on the Brain

Heart on the Brain started with the fundamental question of who we are, and what defines us. This book also raises the question of what it means for a human to be free. This freedom comes with a particular uncertainty of our total responsibility for our choices. Some claim that we are, to some extent, what we choose to be. Choices and the decisions we make shape our lives. But how do we make decisions? By listening to the heart? Is the brain responsible for decision-making? Or both the heart and the brain? How could we define ourselves?

Heart on the Brain will dive into the neuroscientific reasons of how bodily signals, such as our heartbeats, modify brain processes, including, for example, our decisions. Starting with research on the functions of our heart to study the functions of our brain, it will explain the heart-brain interaction. You will get to know your own heart and your own brain, and how they interact.

It will explain how heartache and grace influence the heart dynamics and, consequently, our mental state. The book will show how even the perception of our own heartbeats plays a pivotal role in human decision-making. This book will provide you with methods on how to improve your awareness and enhance well-being and quality of life.

Heart on the Brain will give a new perspective on how we could define ourselves – and challenge all readers to come up with further interpretations.

While this is not an exhaustive study, I hope that it will nonetheless give you a solid enough grounding in the science involved. Perhaps it will leave you wondering just how much you truly know about the world and even about yourself.

Knowing yourself better gives you more freedom to make choices, which makes your life happier. This requires philosophical self-reflection and finding out what makes you *you*. Getting to know your own heart and brain is an even deeper step into knowing yourself.

The scientific groundings of this book are accompanied by art and photography. My experience has shown me that science and art are intertwined. They both encompass our attempts to understand and describe the world both within and around us. When I approach a question about life from a scientific stance, the subjects and methods will take a different form than when I use art to convey my perceptions. However, I always reach the same end: coming to a greater appreciation of the human experience and sharing that understanding with my community.

I am constantly striving to view the world from new perspectives and then communicate my vision to share what I understand of the world. In my scientific research, I conduct experiments over and over again, trying to pin down some new aspect of reality, using traditional modes of communication. When I take an artistic approach, I start with a vision, then explore the ways to convey my message using tactile visuals that others can connect with. Bringing together science, art, and photography, I explore some of the ultimate philosophical questions surrounding human experiences and share my understanding with you.

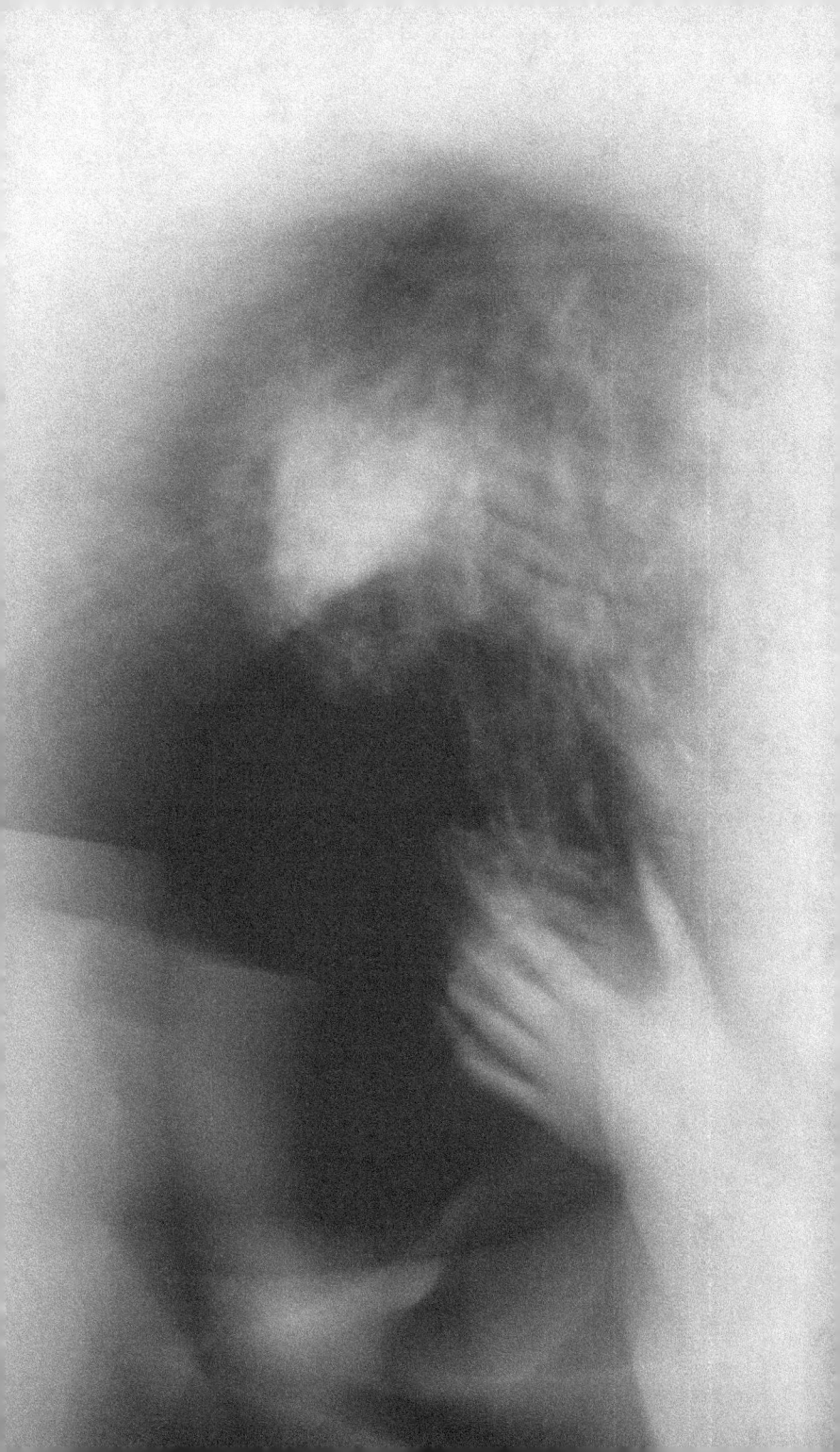

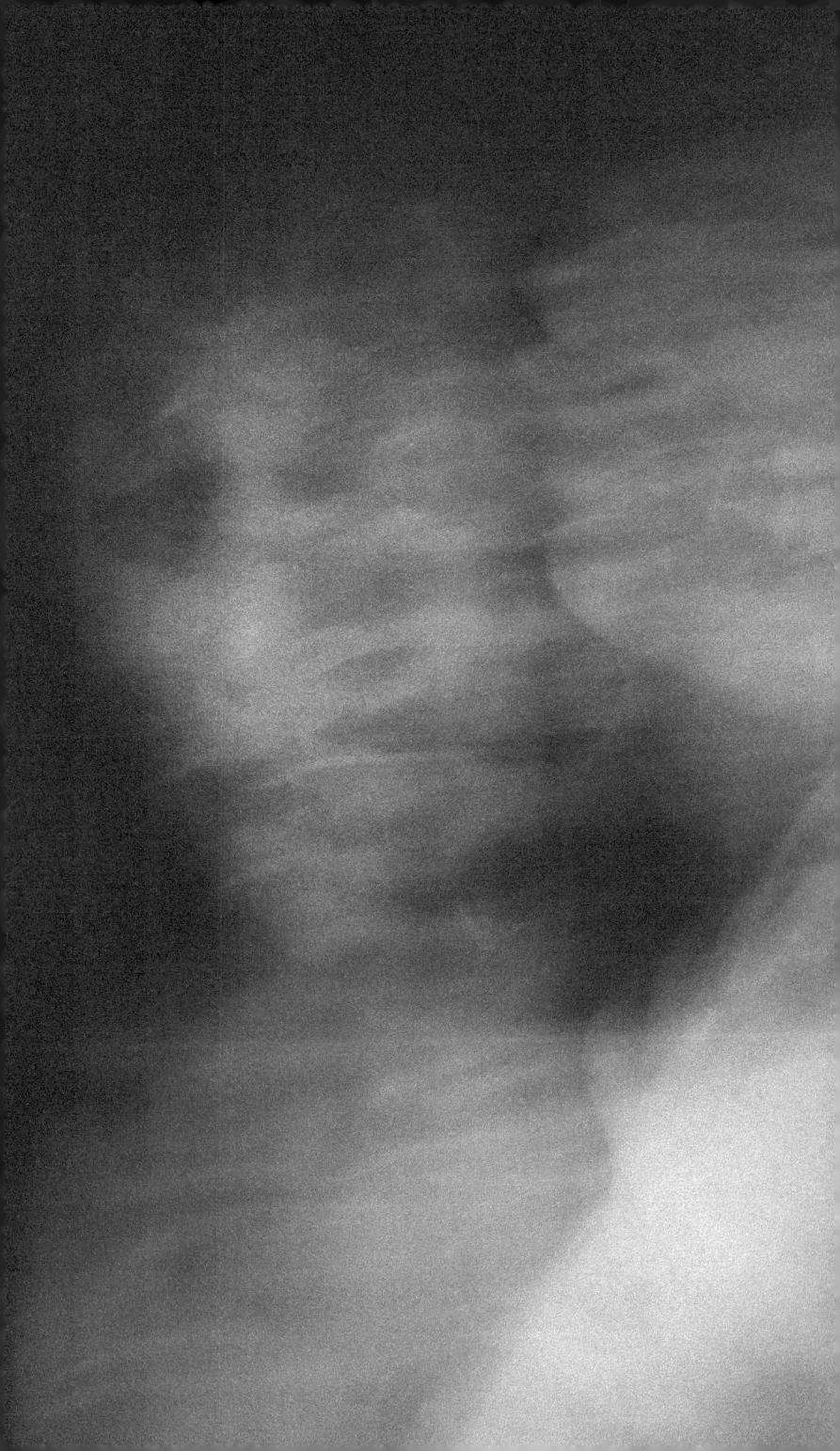

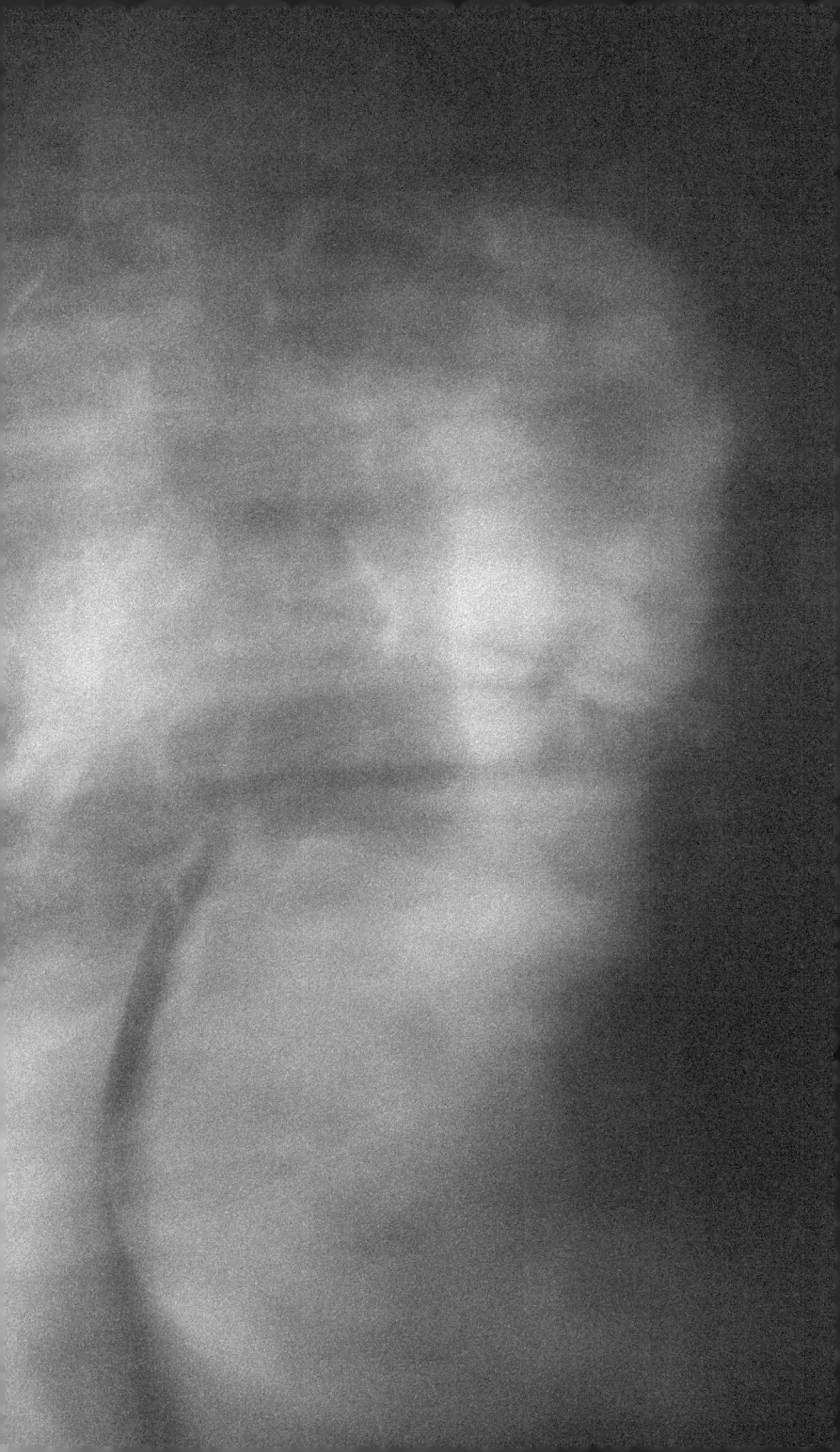

2. KNOW YOUR OWN HEART

Centuries ago, the human heart was regarded as a chamber for the soul. However, the discoveries brought on by the advent of modern science have since revealed that the human heart is a biological pump. The heart has a crucial role in sustaining life – pumping oxygen and nutrients throughout our body. It sustains every single one of our organ systems and ensures that everything is working in perfect unison.

The enduring association between the human heart and human emotions is deeply ingrained into our psyche. When we're frightened, we can feel our heart thundering away in our chest. When we're grieving or overwhelmed, we experience a longing heartache. When we're happy, on the other hand, we have the sensation our heartbeat is fluttering like a butterfly. Evidently, labelling the heart as merely being a biological pump is selling it short.

Aside from pumping blood through our vessels, our heart has an intrinsic role to play when it comes to the way we interact with our internal and external states and how we experience the resulting feelings. The heart and the brain are engaged in a constant two-way dialogue, and the complex emotions we experience in response to stimuli are a result of this dialogue.

For example, when we're feeling stressed, angry or anxious, the rhythm of our heart becomes fast-paced and erratic. Conversely, emotions such as compassion, happiness, and gratitude produce a smoother, more regular rhythm that creates a sensation of tranquillity and warmth. Indeed, the relationship between the heart and our emotions is so powerful that experiencing negative emotional states for an extended period of time can even increase the risk of developing serious health conditions, such as heart disease. Therefore, experiencing more positive feelings can also reduce the likelihood of falling ill and actually improve the health of our heart.

In order to truly understand the emotional function of our heart, it's essential that we take a glimpse into its anatomy.

The Anatomy of the Heart

Scientifically speaking, the heart can be considered to be two hollow organs – the right half and the left half – divided by muscular walls. Each half consists of an atrium and a ventricle. The atria are the heart's two upper chambers, and these thin-walled chambers receive blood from the veins. The ventricles comprise the two lower chambers of the heart, and with their thick, muscular walls, they forcefully pump blood through and out of the heart. Each of these chambers is separated by walls of tissue called the septum. Blood is pumped throughout the chambers by four heart valves that systematically open and close to ensure the blood is flowing between and from the chambers in a single direction.

The right half of the heart receives oxygen-depleted blood from the entire body, sending it to the lungs, where it is re-oxygenated. Once oxygenated, the blood is returned to the left half of the heart, where it is then distributed once again throughout the body's organ systems. Each half has its own distinct role, with the right half pumping out only de-oxygenated blood whilst the left half pumps out only oxygenated blood (Antoni, 1989).

Cardiac cycles refer to the sequence of events occurring from the end of one heartbeat to the beginning of the next. Each cardiac cycle consists of two phases – the systolic (systole) phase and the diastolic (diastole) phase.

Systole refers to when the left and right ventricles contract and pump blood into the aorta and pulmonary valves, respectively. This phase is the period of ventricular contractions and occurs between the first and second heart sounds of the cardiac cycle. During systole, the aortic and pulmonic valves are opened in order to eject blood into the aorta and pulmonary valves. The mitral and tricuspid valves (atrioventricular valves) remain closed, which means that no blood enters the ventricles during systole, although it does continue to enter the atria through the vena cavae and pulmonary veins. It is during systole that arterial blood pressure reaches its peak (systolic blood pressure).

Diastole represents the timeframe wherein the ventricles are relaxed and not contracting, beginning when the aortic and pulmonary valves close. Pressure within the ventricle (intraventricular) falls, but there is little increase in blood volume within the ventricles (ventricular volume). This process is referred to as isovolumetric relaxation. Once the ventricular pressure falls below the pressure of the atria (atrial pressure), the mitral and tricuspid valves open and blood flows passively from the two atria to the two ventricles.

There is initially a significant pressure gradient between the atria and the ventricles, as a result of which the ventricular fills rapidly. Generally, 70% of ventricular filling occurs during this phase. As diastole progresses, the ventricular pressure begins to rise, and the filling rate slows down (in a process called diastasis). Filling is completed during atrial contracting, beginning the transition from ventricular diastole to atrial systole. Once the pressure in the ventricles has risen above the pressure in the atria, the mitral and tricuspid valves close and the diastole is complete (Sidebotham & Le Grice, 2007).

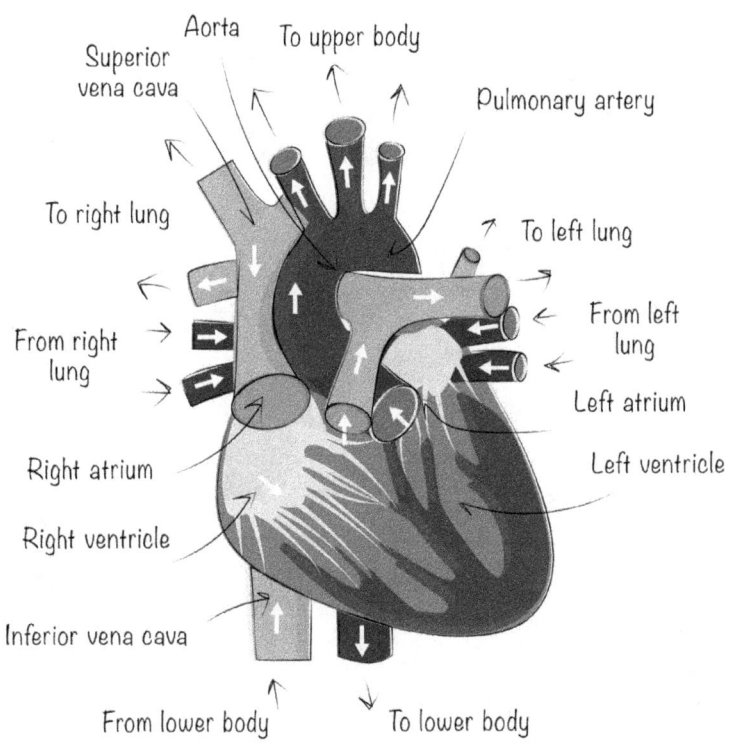

The Electrocardiogram

Your heart's rhythm and electrical activity can be checked with the so-called electrocardiogram (ECG). A sensor is attached to the skin and detects the electrical signal that your heart produces each time it beats. These signals are then recorded by a machine and can be used for investigations. In order to understand the ECG, let us have a look first at the electrical activity of your heart.

The electrocardiogram (ECG) signal basically corresponds to the electrical activity of the heart. In scientific literature, the ECG has been extensively studied and analysed for a variety of purposes, included measuring heart rate, examining the rhythm of heartbeats, diagnosing heart abnormalities, emotional recognition as well as biometric identification.

The procedures for ECG analysis vary depending on the nature and reason of the analysis. They can consist of several steps such as pre-processing, feature extraction, selection and transformation as well as classification. Performing each step chronologically is crucial in order to achieve reliable, accurate and the desired results for the specific analysis. Moreover, employing successful measures and appropriately constituting the ECG signal plays a fundamental role in the analysis as well.

An electrocardiogram (ECG) is the surface recording of the electrical activity of the heart. The P wave corresponds to the depolarization of the atria during the later stages of ventricular diastole. The PR interval is the period from the beginning of atrial activation to the beginning of ventricular activation. The QRS complex corresponds to ventricular depolarization. Meanwhile, the ST segments cover the time frame from when the ventricular myocytes are in phase two (the plateau) of their action potentials. Finally, the T wave represents ventricular repolarization (Sidebotham, 2007).

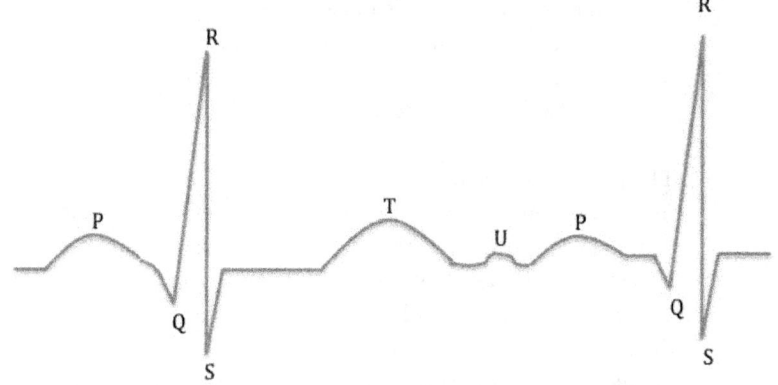

Autonomic Nervous System

Your heart rate, along with other involuntary body processes like blood pressure, respiration, or digestion, is controlled by the autonomic nervous system. Basically, body processes that take place without your conscious effort are taken care of by your autonomic nervous system, or ANS.

The ANS consists of three anatomically distinct divisions; sympathetic, parasympathetic and enteric. Some textbooks do not include the enteric nervous system as part of this system. In this chapter, I will explain only the parasympathetic and the sympathetic nervous system.

The parasympathetic division, or parasympathetic nervous system, is responsible for the body's rest and digestion response. When the body is relaxed and resting, the parasympathetic nervous system is working. The parasympathetic nervous system decreases respiration and heart rate and increases digestion. Therefore, the parasympathetic division is also known as the "rest and digest" process. It lets your heart rest and takes care of your digestions, which is why it is important to give your body enough rest after you have put in the effort.

Activation of the sympathetic division, or the sympathetic nervous system, leads to a state of elevated activity and attention, known as the "fight or flight" response. During this process, your heart beats considerably faster. Under stress conditions, the entire sympathetic nervous system is activated and produces an immediate widespread of responses, making sure you can react to danger, if necessary. The sympathetic nervous system innervates almost every living tissue within the body. During stress, when the sympathetic division is active and your heart rate increases, the stress hormone cortisol secretion also increases. Short amounts of stress are normal, but chronic stress results in a long-term "fight-or-flight", which leads to a constantly increased heart rate and a constant cortisol production. This, in return, is associated with physiological consequences, including illnesses, such as diabetes or even cardiovascular diseases. There are times and seasons for working hard, and there are times to rest and recover. If you find a good balance between the two, it means that the interaction between the parasympathetic and the sympathetic division is also in harmony.

Heart rate variability

"Heart rate" refers to the number of heartbeats per minute. Heart rate variability (HRV) is the fluctuation in time intervals between adjacent heartbeats. A healthy heartbeat is not a consistent metronome. The oscillations of a healthy heart are actually complex and non-linear. The beat-to-beat fluctuations of a healthy heart are most appropriately described as mathematical chaos. The variability of your heart rates provides the body with the flexibility to rapidly cope with uncertain and changing environments.

Let me give you an example. Try to feel your pulse on your wrist while taking a few deep breaths in and out. You might feel how the interval between beats gets longer (that's when the heart rate slows down) when you exhale and shorter (that's when the heart rate increases) when you inhale. Respiration, for example, influences the variability in heart rates.

In addition to respiration, the variability in heart rates is also influenced by exercise, hormonal reactions, metabolic processes, cognitive processes, stress and recovery.

Important to note here is that higher variability in heart rates has been found to be associated with improved psychological well-being and quality of life. This is because HRV should increase during relaxing activities. For example, when you meditate or sleep, then the parasympathetic nervous system (the system responsible for your body's rest) should dominate. On the other hand, HRV naturally decreases during stressful situations, when the sympathetic nervous system is elevated. During stress, your heart beats faster, in order to keep up with the demand. But also, during stress, the variability of your heart rate decreases. This is why sleep and meditation are so important: They increase HRV and make you healthier and happier.

However, a higher HRV is not always healthier, because pathological conditions can also produce HRV. When cardiac conduction abnormalities elevate HRV measurements, this is strongly correlated with an increased risk of mortality (especially among the elderly). Close examinations of ECG morphology can reveal whether elevated HRV values are caused by cardiac problems or whether you are healthy.

The variability of your heart rate doesn't follow a specific pattern either; some circumstances will result in an increase in variation, resulting in high HRV, whilst other situations will cause the time between heartbeats to remain more constant and therefore maintain a low HRV. Heart rate variability is intrinsically connected with the autonomic nervous system (ANS). It can provide in-depth insights into the balance between the parasympathetic (rest and digest system) and sympathetic (fight or flight system) branches of the nervous system.

Although individuals respond uniquely when it comes to HRV levels, it is still an accurate indicator of physical health and well-being. Within sports science, for example, HRV levels have been studied extensively regarding their role in monitoring whether athletes are over-training or if they are experiencing current and accumulated fatigue.

We can use HRV as a good indicator of our health and well-being in sports and generally in life. The HRV level changes naturally, from day to day, based on the level of activity and stress levels. If a person is chronically stressed, the interplay between the two systems (rest/digest and fight/flight) will get disrupted, the body is in a constant fight state, and HRV levels remain low. As a consequence, the body has less resilience to external demands, which can cause mental and health problems.

The key here is trying really hard, then stopping, recovering, and then trying again. This balance will not only create an internal equilibrium and wellbeing in the body, but also keeps your heart healthy. Take time to meditate, sleep well and put in the work when you need to. Your HRV will thank you.

Heartbeat perception

For a moment, try to sit still (or lay down) and try to count your heartbeats without putting your hand on your heart, and without taking your pulse. Can you feel your heartbeat? And on a scale from one to ten, how well can you feel them?

Heartbeat perception, or how you can perceive your own heartbeats without taking the pulse, has been of interest in previous research. Over the years, it has been shown that the perception of our own bodily processes, such as our heartbeats, is coupled to our emotional experiences. It has been deduced that individuals who show a good perception of their own heart activity tend to exhibit higher levels of a momentarily experienced emotion (for example, anxiety, sadness, joy or enjoyment). Thus, the better we can perceive our own heartbeats, the stronger we experience momentary emotions.

To test how well individuals can perceive their own heartbeats, researchers have asked participants to count their own heartbeats silently. The beginning and end of the counting phases were signaled by a start and stop tone. During heartbeat counting, participants should not take their pulse or attempt to use other manipulations facilitating the counting of heartbeats. After the stop signal, participants were required to verbally report the number of counted heartbeats to the researcher, and then the next counting phase started. At the same time, participants were attached to electrodes to record their actual heartbeats via electrocardiography (ECG). Their reported number of heartbeats was then compared to the actual number of beats extracted from the ECG. The difference between the actual heartbeats and their perceived heartbeats was taken as their score on heartbeat perception. The smaller the difference, the better their heartbeat perception.

One of the most prominent researchers in the field of heartbeat perception is Rainer Schandry. For years he has been studying heartbeat-evoked potentials, which are neurotransmissions from the heart to the brain, and has generated some fascinating discoveries. Although I have never met him in person, I have extensively read through his research, studied his papers, and also called a task in my experiment the 'Schandry task'. Rainer Schandry and his colleagues have focused their research on heartbeat perception and the associated mental activity.

The researchers wanted to investigate the extent to which participants could detect their heartbeats without taking their pulse, and how this is correlated with their mental activity. In a study conducted by Pollatos and Schandry (2004), the participants were seated in a sound-attenuated chamber and electrodes were attached to their scalps (electroencephalography/EEG) and heart (electrocardiography/ECG). They were then instructed to count their heartbeats silently over the course of four different counting phases – without actually taking their pulse.

Following a stop signal, the participants were then asked to verbally state the number of counted heartbeats, following which the next phase would commence. They were not informed about the length of the counting phases or regarding their accuracy. The research revealed that the more accurately the participants could detect their heartbeats, the higher the measured amplitude in the brain of this neurotransmission from the heart to the brain (or heartbeat-evoked potential).

Furthermore, there is evidence that feedback from an internal organ is associated with decision-making processes, as investigated by the researchers Werner, Jung, Duschek and Schandry (2009). Participants in this study were categorised as having either an accurate or poor preconception of their heart activity. For the study, the researchers conducted the Iowa Gambling Task, in which participants have to choose between four card decks. Decks A and B yield high gains and high losses, but if they are played continuously result in a net loss. On the other hand, decks C and D yield small gains and small losses but with continuous play result in a net profit.

Participants in this study had to avoid net loss and achieve net gain. The researchers revealed that those participants with an accurate perception of their heartbeat chose significantly more of the net gain and fewer of the net loss options. This conclusion supports and elaborates upon previous findings, suggesting that heartbeat perception is associated with a behavioural advantage. This study demonstrated that perception of somatic feedback (feedback from the body) is correlated with selecting more advantageous options in complex and uncertain situations during the decision-making process. Therefore, the cardiac perception could function as a mediator in behavioural regulation and have a considerable impact in terms of real-life applicability.

The observation that enhanced heartbeat perception is associated with superior decision-making is in accordance with other investigations demonstrating better learning and memory performance in individuals with good cardiac perception. For example, Katkin, Wiens and Öhman (2001) revealed superior classical conditioning in those with good heartbeat perception. In their study, accurate and poor heartbeat perceivers were presented with backward-masked images of fear-inducing stimuli. Presenting backward-masked images means presenting one visual stimulus (a "mask" or "masking stimulus") immediately after a brief "target" visual stimulus, which results in a failure to consciously perceive the first stimulus. Some of these visual stimuli were consistently followed by an electric shock. The researchers found that individuals with good heartbeat perception were able to predict shock occurrence much more accurately than those with poor heartbeat perception.

Pollatos and Schandry (2008) demonstrated improved recognition performance of previously presented pleasant and unpleasant pictures in participants with good cardiac perception, unlike their less perceptive counterparts. Other studies have also indicated that cardiac perception has a significant influence on emotional processing. Individuals with good cardiac perception tend to demonstrate more intense emotional experiences when exposed to picture stimuli, film clips, or emotion-related adjectives, as well as reporting higher anxiety (Ferguson & Katkin, 1996; Herbert, Pollatos et al., 2007; Pollatos, Gramann et al., 2007; Pollatos, Herbert, Matthias et al., 2007; Pollatos, Traut-Mattausch et al., 2007; Schandry, 1981).

Traditionally, visual perception, spatial awareness and emotion have been considered separate areas of study. The research outlined above, however, combines these various fields and, as a result, creates intriguing and fascinating lines of scientific inquiry and discovery. With regards to health, pathology, and mortality, there are considerable implications resulting from these studies. For example, the relationship between HRV and the ANS means that someone experiencing consistently lower levels of HRV is also experiencing an activated sympathetic 'fight or flight' response. For someone with poor cardiac perception, failing to recognize this suppressed parasympathetic activity could lead to the inability of their body to engage in recovery mode, cause a prolonged negative emotional state, or result in inefficient metabolic activity leading to altered eating behaviours.

With regards to cardiac perception, studies conducted by researchers have demonstrated that the human heart has an even more significant role in our lives than it has ever been given credit for. Besides being a biological pump, our heart not only responds to and elicits emotional responses to internal and external stimuli, but it also provides a pathway for our emotions to influence perception. The implications of such observations are vast; they indicate that our heart impacts the way in which we see, interact with, and respond to the input generated by our senses.

Essentially, this is implying our perceptual systems are so intricately interconnected and interdependent that our emotional states influence our perception, which then, in turn, influences our cognition. Considering that our heart has a major role in the way we determine emotions and feelings, this would also mean that our heart, to a considerable extent, determines the ways in which we interpret the world around us, our interactions, and our experiences. Psychology has revealed that our cognitive processes and thoughts create the beliefs, values, attitudes, and behaviours that make us who we are as individuals. If our heart influences these cognitive processes, then our heart also influences those aspects of ourselves, making us individual, unique, and human.

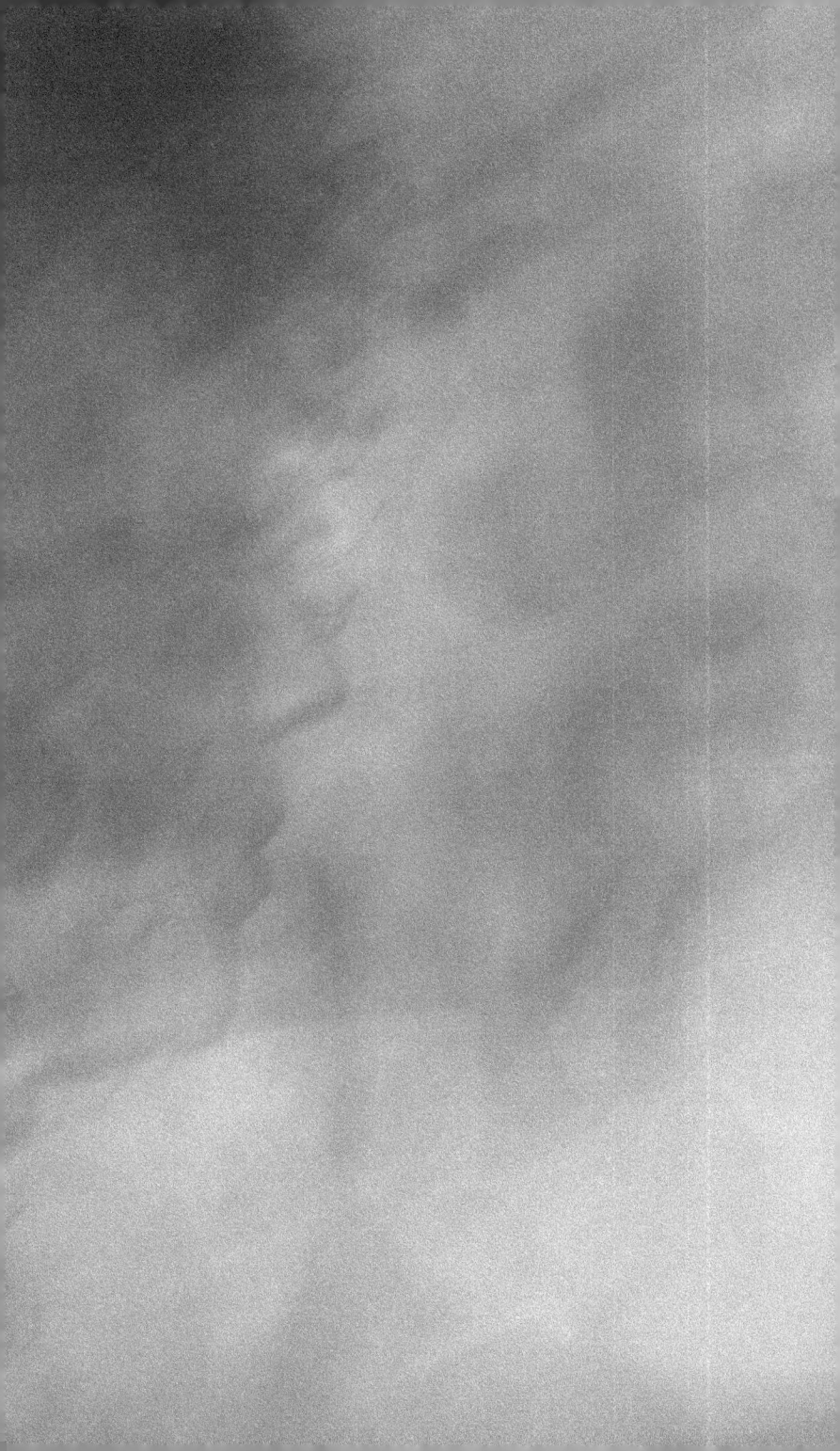

3. KNOW YOUR BRAIN

The heart evidently has a role to play in our experiences, emotions, and actions. However, focusing only on the heart at the expense of the brain will restrict us from truly understanding our human consciousness. Our experiences, interpretations, beliefs, values and subsequent attitudes, decisions and choices all arise from the mental processes which go on in our brains.

As the command centre for our nervous system, our brain receives signals as electronic impulses from our body's sensory organs and then relays the information to our muscles. Essentially, human consciousness would be impossible without the brain. Composed of billions of nerve cells, countless nerve fibres and literally trillions of connections, our brain is the driving centre for our perceptions of the world, the ways in which we interpret our experiences, our memories, and our sense of self and identity, as well as the choices we make and their resulting actions.

Every major and minor system within our body is regulated by this highly sophisticated and specialised organ. It not only directs our body's internal functions but integrates sensory impulses from the outside world and the information coming from our internal thoughts and observations. Whilst it weighs only three pounds, our brain is the source of our entire consciousness and – by extension – what it is to be human.

Our brain is divided into four major sections. The four lobes of the brain are the frontal, parietal, temporal, and occipital lobes. The parietal lobe, which sits right at the top of the brain, is responsible for integrating sensory information and language, which is necessary for our short-term memory, for example. The frontal lobe is the section that sits at the front of the brain, behind the forehead. This part of the brain is responsible for higher cognitive functions such as thinking, planning, and reasoning. The prefrontal cortex, the very front part of the frontal lobe, is assigned particular credit for complex thinking and is associated with abilities such as planning complex behaviour and decision-making.

The ventromedial prefrontal cortex (vmPFC) is a part of the prefrontal cortex. It is implicated in the processing of risk and fear, as it is critical in the regulation of amygdala activity in humans. It also plays a role in the inhibition of emotional responses, the process of decision making and self-control, and the cognitive evaluation of morality.

The amygdala is one of two almond-shaped clusters of nuclei located deep within the temporal lobes of the brain. It is shown to perform a primary role in processing memory, decision-making, and emotional responses, including fear, anxiety, and aggression.

In order to be able to think, act, judge and decide, we need to be able to do a tremendous number of things at once – we need to be able to perceive many things simultaneously and sort through them, and we need to be able to integrate that information into our existing memory schemas so that we can understand what it is we are seeing or remembering. Made up of billions of neurons (or nerve cells) that communicate in trillions of connections called synapses, I think it's fair to say that your brain is one of the most complex and fascinating organs in your body.

Parts of the Human Brain

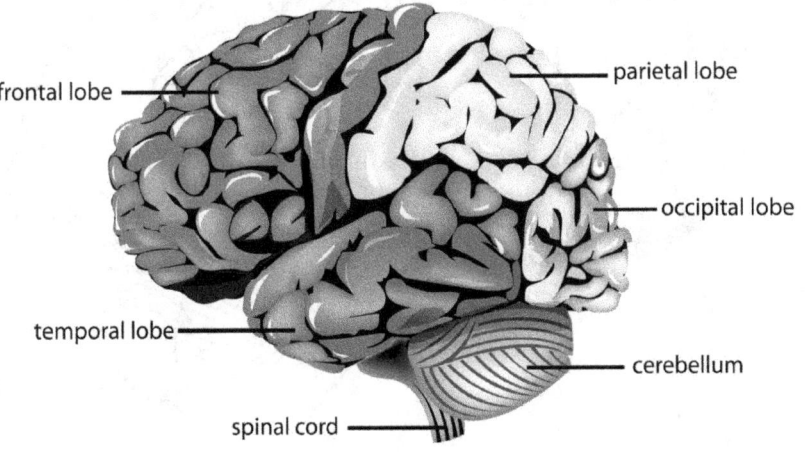

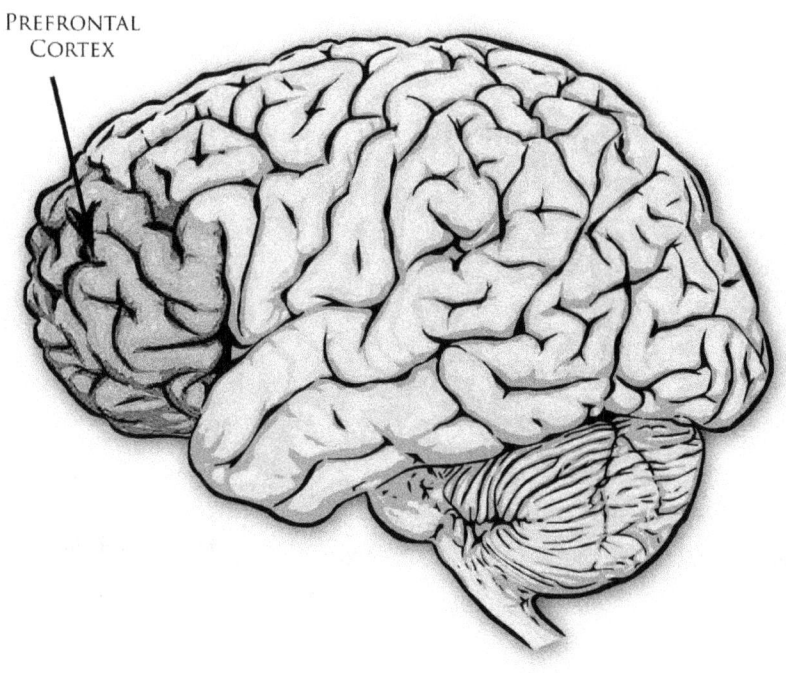

Plastic Brains

A question that has fascinated us ever since we first began to entertain the idea that there might be no such thing as a spirit, is the question of how we are able to store and experience our thoughts.

If the spirit or the soul is seen as an extension of the brain, all information must be stored physically in the brain. This movement away from dualism (the belief that the mind and body are separate) to monism (the belief that all thinking originates in the brain) has led to an immense desire to understand the physical workings of the brain.

The philosopher Descartes believed that the soul and body interacted through the so-called pineal gland, a pea-sized structure located close to the centre of the brain. Nowadays, most scientists agree that our consciousness is not related to an incorporeal spirit. Our consciousness seems to be the result of a complex array of physical systems that are working together.

Thanks to modern technology, including brain-imaging procedures such as fMRI (functional magnetic resonance imaging) and EEG (electroencephalography), we can now examine active brains while they are perceiving the world.

An fMRI scanner looks similar to an MRI scanner, on which you lay down to scan your body. Instead of scanning your body, fMRI scans the brain and may be used to examine the brain's functional anatomy. Functional magnetic resonance imaging (fMRI) measures brain activity by detecting changes associated with blood flow. This technique relies on the fact that blood flowing through the brain and neuronal activation are coupled. When an area of the brain is in use, blood flow to that brain region increases. As you engage in different activities, from simple tasks to complex ones, the activity of the neurons constantly fluctuates. Even when you rest quietly, the brain is still highly active, and the patterns of activity are thought to reveal particular networks of areas that often act together. Thanks to fMRI scans, we can map these brain activities.

Another technique is the electroencephalography (EEG). EEG detects electrical activity in your brain using small metal discs (electrodes) attached to your scalp. Your brain cells constantly communicate via electrical impulses and are active all the time, even when you're sleeping. This activity can be recorded and appears as wavy lines (which are the different wave frequencies) on an EEG recording. While EEG is helpful for diagnosing brain disorders, it is also frequently used in research settings to study these "wavy lines". When you are in a fully conscious but relaxed state, for example, you would have regularly recurring oscillating waves known as alpha waves. When you are excited, the alpha waves are replaced by rapid, irregular waves. During sleep, your brain waves become extremely slow. Brain waves change according to the situation at hand.

Our brains are also incredibly adaptive. They are created for a world of uncertainty and quick decision-making, having had to survive in harsh environments since their inception.

The adaptive quality of our brain is called neuronal plasticity, and it is only due to neuronal plasticity that we can have memories, learn, judge and decide to our advantage. The cells in our brain, called neurons, connect with one another to develop meaningful networks, and these networks change in accordance with new experiences. If we were unable to incorporate further information into our existing neural networks, we would be unable to change our thinking or behaviour in light of new evidence, and we would be hard-pressed to deal with any alteration to our environment.

It is also through this process that we are able to record and incorporate both the positive and negative experiences we have with others, and this can ultimately help us differentiate friend from foe, good from bad, advantageous from non-advantageous.

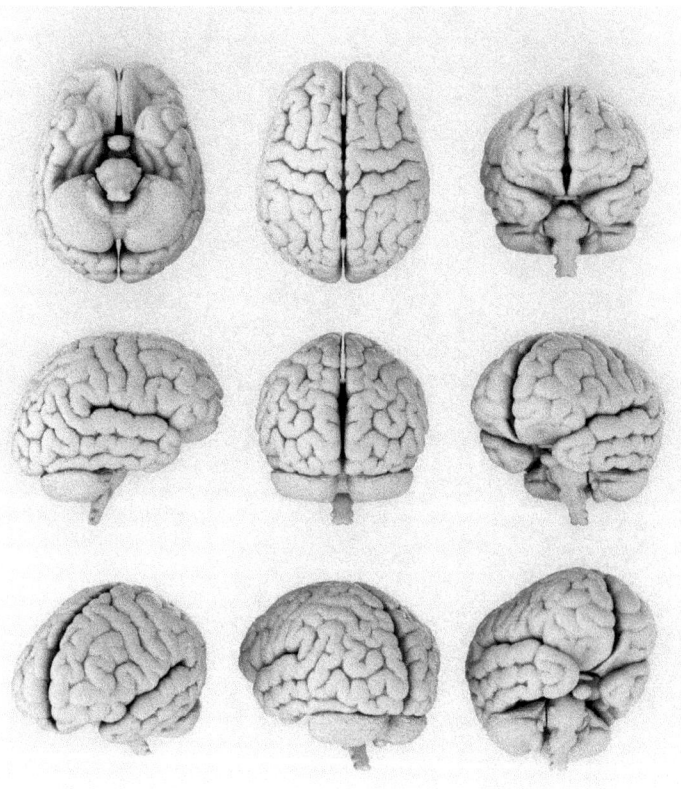

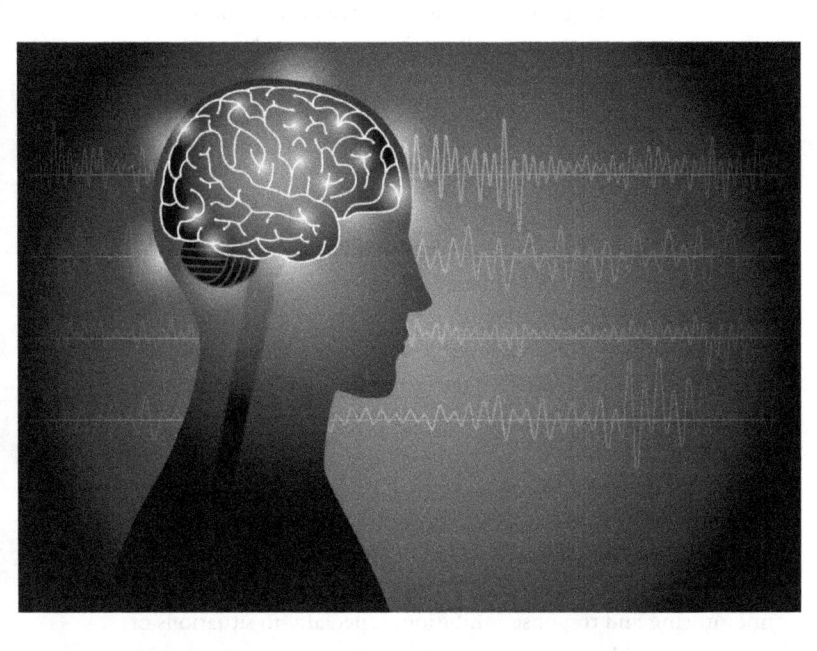

Decision-Making

Although our brain is responsible for making decisions in our life, many emotional factors can affect its rational ability. Our brain and heart are connected, responsible for changing our ability to make rational or emotional decisions.

When we send a sign to our brain that "we have to make a decision," the body as an overall machine must work together to define the result. The brain will look for past experiences and decide based on our past experiences, emotions, and how those factors have affected us as humans, and also how those actions and reactions define us as individuals.

Brain mechanisms in decision making were obtained from research in brain-damaged patients and normal subjects with functional neuroimaging studies, that have led to the identification of the neural structures involved in decision making in humans. The main region involved in decision making is the ventromedial prefrontal cortex, which integrates relevant sensory and emotional information. Other structures involved in the various relevant processes in decision making include the amygdala and the cingulate cortex. The amygdala processes and encodes the emotional signal and its association with contextual stimuli. The cingulate cortex is responsible for the processes of monitoring and response inhibition, especially in situations of uncertainty (Martínez-Selva et al., 2006).

By making decisions and choosing our path, we also continuously choose who we are and who we will become in the future. Every action has a reaction, and once the brain makes that decision, it is on us to understand why the brain is making that decision and why that chosen option.

Choosing to get married, or not, to have children, or not, and selecting a field of study or profession are all part of discovering who we are as individuals and who we want to be. It is why we may argue that we are what we choose to be, or the sum of our past and current decisions.

Understanding the dynamics of how our brain works when it comes to decision making, knowing that there are always consequences, will help us evolve as humans and develop more ability to make wiser decisions in our life.

According to researchers, our brain makes a decision before we even realize it. Most of our decisions are made unconsciously, and the fact that the brain decides without our "approval" proves that our past experiences are heavily responsible for defining our future. An experiment conducted by Benjamin Libet validates this theory. Libet et al. (1983) measured the time when subjects became consciously aware of the decision to move.

In the Libet Experiment, test subjects were hooked up to a brain scanner and asked to flex their wrists whenever they wanted to. Also, they were asked to watch a special clock and record the time at which they made each decision to flex.

What Libet found is that test subjects reported that they decided to flex on average about 0.15 seconds before their muscles actually flexed. However, their brain showed signs of "ramping up" to flex (known as the "Readiness Potential") on average, about 0.55 seconds before their muscles flexed.

They concluded that the brain shows signs of being about to produce muscle motion before we report that we are aware of having made the decision to move our muscles. We tend to decide before consciously thinking about the decision we make.

Libet and his colleagues made fundamental discoveries relating to timing factors in producing a freely voluntary act (Libet, 2002). Based on some of the results discussed in the previous paragraphs, it appears that what may seem to be a freely made decision is actually a decision that is made unconsciously before one is consciously aware of having made that decision.

Making decisions is a part of everyday life. A lot of information is out there about how to become better decision-makers, focusing on aspects, such as identifying a decision, gathering information, assessing alternative resolutions, and so forth. The majority of advice actually focuses on information, knowledge, checklists, or unrealistic solutions, which promise you will become more successful and happier.

Understanding and identifying the problem, generating possible solutions, evaluating the pros and cons, making a decision, implementing the option chosen and then assessing the impact are all part of the decision-making process.

Although knowing the decision-making process itself does not guarantee a successful result, being aware of what is happening inside and outside us is crucial to get to know ourselves as humans. Look to the core of your feelings and emotions, how your body reacts to outside stimuli and how your brain responds to that.

Acknowledging how our brain works, how the decision-making process works and how internal and external influences can modify our decisions and our behaviours, is the first step to start moulding ourselves as individuals.

It is how we will evolve our ability to make wiser decisions for our future. It is how we learn how to make decisions that will help us to grow as individuals.

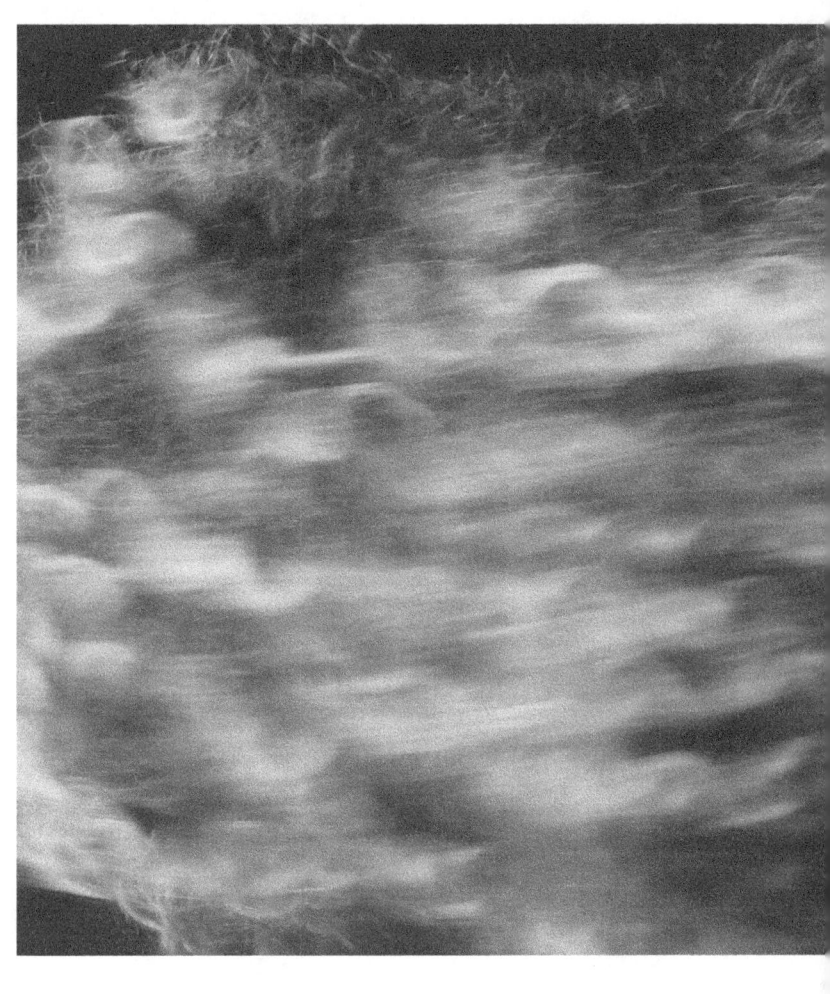

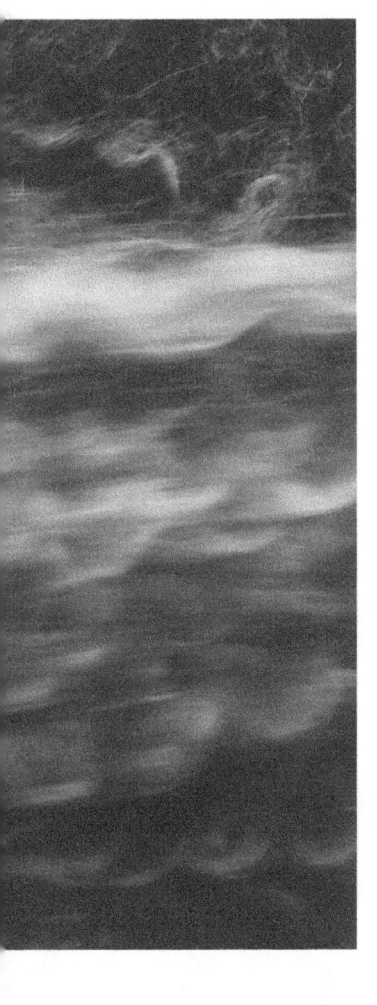

4. THE HEART-BRAIN INTERACTION

The heart-brain connection has been the subject of much research, which has aimed to find the correlation between the two and how it affects our lives. The connection is truly dynamic and interdependent, with the heart and the brain regularly communicating with one another and the heart influencing the brain's ability to make decisions.

Scientifically, the brain is directly connected to the heart by the sympathetic and parasympathetic branches of the autonomic nervous system and vice versa. This means that impulses and signals received by the brain will be felt within the heart, and sensations and responses within the heart will be sent to the brain. Without one, the other would be incomplete.

Inspired by case studies of brain lesion patients such as Phineas Gage, one of the most famous brain injury survivors, neuroscientist Antonio Damasio proposes the Somatic Marker hypothesis, stating how emotions play an essential role in decision making (Damasio, 1994). The term "somatic" refers to the body and brain-related signals, which we experience as emotions and feelings.

The fundamental viewpoint of this hypothesis is that when the outcomes of a decision are unclear or ambiguous to the brain, feelings and emotions can take over. The brain's ability to maintain its internal equilibrium is essential to making the best decisions.

The ventromedial prefrontal cortex (vmPFC) is critical for triggering various bodily changes in response to stimuli, such as cues for reward or punishment. As we make decisions under uncertainty, our assessment of their immediate and future potential consequences may trigger numerous responses that conflict with each other – a highly favourable possible outcome may trigger excitement and elation. In contrast, an aversive result may trigger pain and dread. The result, though, is the emergence of an overall positive or negative signal – basically a "go" or "stop" signal (Damasio, 1994).

Damasio has proposed that numerous and conflicting signals may be triggered simultaneously when keyed up; however, the stronger ones overtake the weaker ones in most cases. In this way, emotional processes are critical for decision making that is advantageous in the long run. However, people deprived of appropriate emotional signals – for example, due to damage to the vmPC in the brain – may fail to perceive potential adverse long-term consequences (Bechara, Tranel, & Damasio, 2000).

Essentially, when it comes to the ability of the brain to make decisions, too little emotion can be as bad as too much emotion. The conflict can compromise the choices made, affecting the emotions and cognition. Wise decision-making happens when the body and the heart are balanced.

The interaction between emotion and cognition also takes centre stage in the work of Damasio, whose "Somatic Marker" hypothesis has been among the most influential theories of emotion in recent years. Essentially, this theory presupposes that feelings and emotions give rise to "bodily markers."

The bodily markers serve as signals helping lead the behaviour in specific directions. One great example is how a rapid heartbeat can be associated with anxiety and can thus influence the subsequent decision-making, resulting, for example, in not taking a particular risk or avoiding a difficult task because of fear. Within the brain, these somatic markers are thought to be processed in the very frontal part of the brain (ventromedial prefrontal cortex) and the amygdala (located within the temporal lobes, see chapter 2).

Researchers have shown that people who are deprived of these somatic markers often lose the ability to experience appropriate emotional responses to different stimuli and occurrences. With the absence of emotions, we cannot make appropriate decisions, leading to socially inappropriate behaviour.

Also known as mind-body interaction, the somatic markers can affect not only perceptions and emotions, but also affect bodily functions in different ways. For example, they influence functions such as heart rate, blood pressure, or muscle contractions; conversely, bodily functions influence the individual's mental state and mood.

According to Damasio (1994, 1999), "somatic markers are emotional reactions with a strong somatic component that supports decision-making, including rational decision making."

These reactions are based upon the individual's previous experiences with similar situations. The somatic markers use a quick preselection of appropriate options, subject to a more detailed cognitive processing for the final decision.

Somatic makers increase the efficiency and accuracy of human decision making. In simple words, if detailed cognitive processing of all the available alternatives were necessary, the brain's ability to make a decision would be almost non-existent.

> "... there are organism states in which the regulation of life processes becomes efficient, or even optimal, free-flowing and easy. This is a well-established physiological fact. It is not a hypothesis. The feelings that usually accompany such physiologically conducive states are deemed "positive," characterized not just by the absence of pain but by varieties of pleasure. There also are organism states in which life processes struggle for balance and can even be chaotically out of control. The feelings that usually accompany such states are deemed "negative," characterized not just by the absence of pleasure but by varieties of pain. ...

> *The fact that we, sentient and sophisticated creatures, call certain feelings positive and other feelings negative is directly related to the fluidity or strain of the life process."*
> (Damasio, 2003, p. 131).

In his work *Looking for Spinoza: Joy, Sorrow and the Feeling Brain*, Antonio Damasio shares his experience with neurological patients to examine the cerebral processes of human emotion. It reveals the biology of our sophisticated survival mechanisms.

When an individual develops his or her perception of how his or her own heartbeat is interconnected to the emotions, this individual understands it directly influences the ability to make decisions.

Studies have shown that individuals who can better perceive their own heartbeats can make better decisions. Let us have a look into heartbeat perception, or how well an individual can perceive his or her own heartbeats by just sitting still and without taking the pulse.

One common observation is that there are substantial interindividual differences in heartbeat perception. The ability to perceive heartbeat activity seems to depend on such factors as gender, percentage of body fat, and physical fitness (Cameron, 2001; Jones, 1994). Significant differences in heartbeat perception ability were also observed in different clinical samples: There is a tendency toward lower perception scores in patients with depressive, somatoform, and personality disorders (Mussgay, Klinkenberg, & Rüddel, 1999), whereas more accurate heartbeat perception has been reported in panic patients (Ehlers, Margraf, & Roth, 1988; Ehlers, Mayou, Sprigings, & Birkhead, 2000). Patients suffering from arrhythmias and benign palpitations (Ehlers et al., 2000) and patients with diabetic neuropathy (Leopold & Schandry, 2001) showed a decreased heartbeat perception ability compared to healthy controls.

Also, Werner et al. (2009) have shown that enhanced cardiac perception is associated with benefits in decision-making.

In their study, Werner et al. (2009) provided empirical evidence that viscero-sensory feedback from an internal organ is associated with decision-making processes. They recruited participants with accurate vs poor perception of their heart activity and compared them with regard to their performance in the Iowa Gambling Task. During the Iowa Gambling Task, participants have to choose between four card decks. Decks A and B yield high gains and high losses, and if played continuously, result in net loss. In contrast, decks C and D yield small gains and small losses, resulting in net profit if they are selected continuously. Thus, participants have to learn to avoid the net loss options favouring the net gain options.

In their study, participants with good cardiac perception chose significantly more of the net gain and fewer of the net loss options. Their findings document the substantial role of feedback coming from bodily signals in decision-making processes in complex situations.

As Damasio in his Somatic Marker hypothesis (Damasio et al., 1991; Damasio, 1994, 1996) states, the bodily signs are correlated to the brain process. In summary, the better we can perceive physical signals, including our own heartbeats, the better we make decisions.

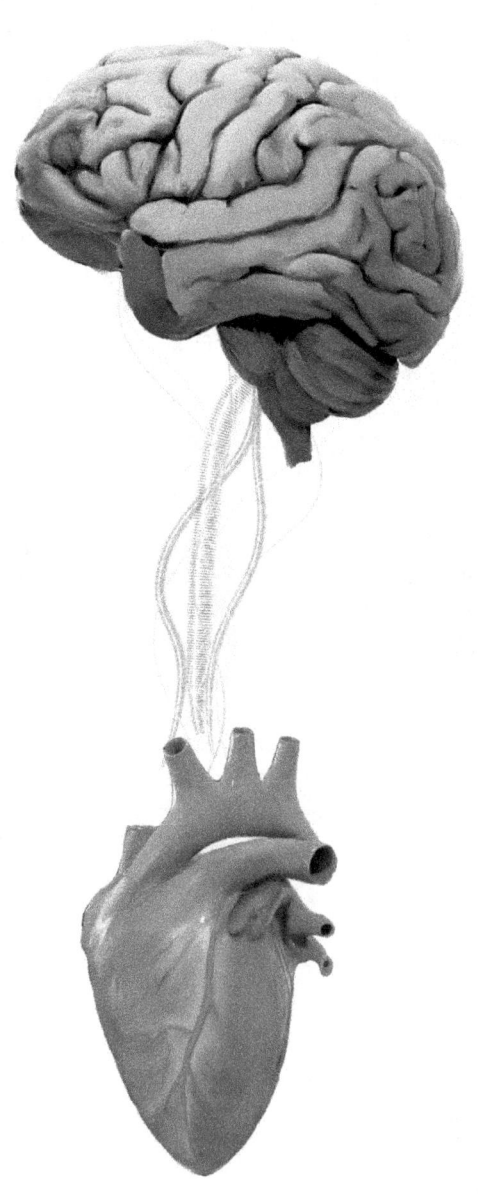

The Somatic Marker Hypothesis

Mental processes related to visceral activity have gained growing interest during the last few years. Damasio's somatic marker hypothesis (Bechara, Damasio, & Damasio, 2000; Damasio, 1994, 2000) is an example of a modern psychological theory incorporating the feedback from the somatosensory and visceral periphery to the cortex. Its fundamental idea is that many mental processes are influenced by "marker" signals arising through bioregulatory processes. Somatic markers are represented and regulated in the emotion circuitry of the brain, particularly in the ventromedial prefrontal cortex (Bechara, Damasio & Damasio, 2000; Bechara, Tranel & Damasio, 2000; Damasio & Damasio 1996).

Damasio's theory emphasizes the importance of the feedback of somatic signals in guiding behaviour and decision-making processes. While making a decision, somatic signals arise from the periphery, including from the viscera, which constitute a specific somatic state related to a specific response option. When choosing between several options, somatic markers have to be developed for each of the options, which requires new learning, and thus performance cannot successfully result from prior knowledge and habitual responses. When new learning is required, cardiovascular activity is established. This association is stored in memory and guides future decision-making (Damasio, 1994, 1996). Particularly in situations of uncertainty and complexity, which do not permit the use of logical analyses, individuals with good cardiac perception can profit from somatic markers previously associated with similar circumstances.

In addition to the somatic markers, the cortical processing of signals from the cardiovascular system was investigated by using a heartbeat-evoked potential (HEP). Heartbeat-evoked potentials (HEPs), neurotransmissions from the heart to the brain, were first addressed by Schandry, Sparrer, and Weitkunat (1986) and have been reported to appear mainly over two brain regions, the somatosensory cortex and the frontal/prefrontal cortex, which is in accordance with knowledge from neuroanatomy (Nieuwenhuys, Voogd, & Van Huijzen, 1988). The influence of the ability to detect one's heartbeats based on the HEP was examined during a heartbeat perception task. The HEP amplitude at the right central location was found to significantly higher in good heartbeat perceivers, confirming that the accuracy of heartbeat perception is reflected in the amplitude of the HEP (Pollatos & Schandry, 2004).

In line with previous research concerning somatic markers and cortical processing of signals from the heart, there is empirical evidence that viscero-sensory feedback from an internal organ is associated with cognitive processing, including mainly decision-making processes (Werner et al., 2009). Participants with accurate versus poor perception of their heart activity were compared with regard to their performance on a computer-based decision-making task. Participants with good cardiac perception chose significantly more of the net gain and fewer of the net loss options (Werner et al., 2009). This documents the substantial role of visceral feedback in cognitive processes and decision-making in complex situations.

The Heart-Brain Coherence

You are aware now that the heart actually sends signals to the brain (and vice versa). These heart signals have a significant effect on brain functions, among others, influencing emotional processing, but also memory or problem-solving. Not only does the heart respond to the brain, but the brain continuously responds to the heart.

You are also aware now how patterns of heart activity have distinct effects on cognitive and emotional function. During stress and generally negative emotions, when the heart rhythm pattern is erratic, the corresponding pattern of neural signals traveling from the heart to the brain inhibits higher cognitive functions, limiting our ability to think clearly, remember, learn, reason, and make effective decisions. Therefore, it is probably not a good idea to make decisions under stress.

On the other hand, the more stable pattern of the heart's input to the brain during positive emotional states facilitates cognitive/brain functions and reinforces positive feelings and emotional stability. Learning to generate increased heart rhythm coherence by sustaining positive emotions, not only benefits the entire body but also profoundly affects how we perceive, think, feel, and perform.

You are aware now that your heart has a naturally occurring beat-to-beat variation in heart rate, the so-called heart rate variability (HRV). The normal variability in heart rate is due to the interaction of the two branches of the autonomic nervous system. The sympathetic nerves act to accelerate heart rate, while the parasympathetic (vagus) nerves slow it down. The sympathetic and parasympathetic branches of the autonomic nervous system are continually interacting to maintain cardiovascular activity in its optimal range and permit appropriate reactions to changing external and internal conditions.

Your beat-to-beat variation seems to be an important indicator of health and fitness. As a marker of physiological resilience and behavioural flexibility, it reflects our ability to adapt effectively to stress and environmental demands. Under a stressor, your heart rate has to go up, and when you are meant to recover, it should go down.

Many factors affect the activity of the autonomic nervous system, and therefore influence the beat-to-beat rhythm, called heart rate variability. These include our breathing patterns, physical exercise, and even our thoughts. Emotions such as anger, frustration, and anxiety give rise to heart rhythm patterns that appear irregular. This pattern indicates that the signals produced by the two branches of the autonomic system (ANS) are out of synchrony. The incoherent patterns of physiological activity associated with these negative emotions can cause our body to operate inefficiently, which takes a lot of our energy.

On the other hand, when we experience positive and uplifting emotions such as appreciation, joy, care, and love, our heart rhythm pattern becomes highly ordered and harmonious. This is called a coherent heart rhythm pattern. When generating a coherent heart rhythm, the activity in the two branches of the ANS is synchronised, and the body's systems operate with increased efficiency and harmony. Positive emotions not only feel, but they also help our body's systems synchronise and work in unison.

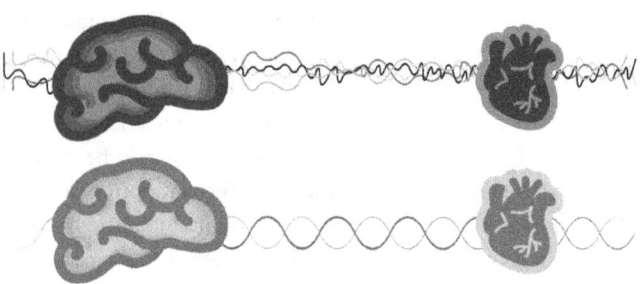

Coherence is associated with a relative increase in parasympathetic activity and encompasses a key element of the relaxation response. However, it is physiologically distinct from relaxation.

The coherence state does not necessarily involve a lowering of heart rate or a change in the amount of HRV, but rather is marked by a change in the heart rhythm pattern. This is different during relaxation, where the heart rate is lowering.

Also, the psychological characteristics of coherence and relation are different. Relaxation is a low-energy state in which the individual rests the body and the mind. Coherence involves the active engagement of positive emotions. Psychologically, coherence is experienced as a balanced, but energized and responsive state that is conducive to everyday functioning, including, for example, the performance of tasks requiring mental focus, problem-solving, and decision-making, as well as physical activity.

So, we have seen now that many of the changes in bodily function that occur during the coherence state revolve around changes in the heart's activity pattern. Historically, the heart has been described as a source of wisdom, spiritual insight, thought, and emotion. However, scientific research over the past decades has begun to expand its understanding of the heart and the role of this amazing organ. Scientists have discovered what they call the "heart brain", which can sense, process information, and make decisions. In essence, it appears that the heart is truly an intelligent system.

The heart seems to be a key component of the emotional system. It does not only respond to emotion; the signals generated by the heart's rhythmic activity actually play a major part in determining the quality of our emotional experience from moment to moment. These heart signals impact cognitive function by virtue of the heart's interaction with the brain.

Understanding Our Consciousness

Throughout life, we find ourselves constantly challenged by our environment, relationships, and the decisions and actions we choose and their resulting consequences. One thing which is a certainty, however, is ourselves. Externally, things may come and go, but we will be living with ourselves for the rest of our lives. The internal conversations which go on in our subconscious are the most important forms of communication we will ever engage in.

This is the dialogue between our heart and brain, driven by the emotional signals they exchange between one another. By listening to this dialogue, you can tap into the natural power and enlightenment of your human consciousness. Listen to the conversations between your heart and brain. Explore your passions and dreams to the fullest. Know yourself so well that even in challenging moments, your focus never waivers.

We are and always will be a work in progress, which is the beauty of being human. As long as our hearts are beating inside of us and our brains are working, then our body and soul will function in wonderful unison and in perfect synchrony. We are always creating and redefining ourselves through our experiences and actions. The heart-brain connection is a spring containing the waters of consciousness, and if we learn to listen to this dialogue, then we will be able to see our reflection and truly understand ourselves with clarity and insight.

We all have a heart and a brain working in unison. This makes us all alike and yet unique simultaneously.

5. WE FEEL, THEREFORE WE ARE

But what are the effects of bodily signals, also known as feelings, on our existence? How could this correlation between heart and brain, body and mind, affect our life and our ability to make decisions?

When we start to understand how our origins and past experiences mould us into what we are today, we understand how our decisions will affect our future. Understanding the consequences of decision-making and how we feel is essential to understand our existence.

When I started researching neuroscience and trying to understand this correlation better, I went back to the 17th century, to French Philosophy. Known as the first great philosopher in the era of "modern philosophy," René Descartes (1596–1650), whose view is called "substance dualism," stated that our minds and our bodies are two different substances. While the body is material (corporeal), the mind is immaterial (incorporeal).

This view leaves room for human souls, who are versed as immaterial. Descartes argued that souls are intangible and can exist separate from the body. He also emphasized that the mind alone is immaterial, whereas the other traditional functions of the souls can be explained as corporeal operations.

The "Cartesian dualism," also referred to as substance dualism, defends the body's idea of existing with two fundamental bases: mental and physical. In his explanation of the mind, the soul, and human's ability to understand the world around them through the powers of their minds, Descartes remains one of the most influential figures not just in modern philosophy, but throughout the history of philosophy.

Descartes' vision was not unanimous, especially in the contemporary era, when philosophers such as Gilbert Ryle (1900-1976) started questioning his views. Gilbert Ryle discussed Cartesian dualism and asserted that the body and mind would not communicate with each other if they were, indeed, distinct. The British philosopher criticises the Cartesian dualism theory of the dissociation of mind and body, which he calls "the dogma of the ghost in the machine." According to Ryle, the acts of learning, remembering, imagining, knowing, and willing are not merely clues to hidden mental processes. Ryle explains that the mind's workings as it governs the body are neither an independent nor a distinct mechanism. He states that there is no entity called "the mind" inside a mechanical apparatus called "the body," but that the mind's modus operandi can be conceptualised as the actions of the body.

Like Gilbert Ryle, many other philosophers, health practitioners and scientists have rejected the Dualism theory by Descartes; yet his theory still somehow seems to be alive.

The French phenomenological philosopher Maurice Jean Jacques Merleau-Ponty (March 1908–3 May 1961) gives, in his work *The Concept of Mind* (*Phénoménologie de la perception*, 1945), detailed descriptions and analyses of bodily experiences. The body's topic is so central that the work is often presented, not as an inquiry into perception, but as a theory of a corporeal, bodily subject.

Merleau-Ponty states that the usual understanding of Descartes as a dualist is biased. He claims that there is a "secret equilibrium" in Descartes' metaphysics, an internal restriction. Still, we fail to see it, for we embrace only one side or aspect of his teaching: "Our science and our philosophy are two faithful and unfaithful consequences of Cartesianism, two monsters born from its dismemberment" (Merleau-Ponty, 1964, 58/177).

We can see Merleau-Ponty developing his view in *Phénoménologie* at the end of the extensive first part titled *Le corps*. There, Merleau-Ponty first makes a summary of his preparatory criticism of empiricist and intellectualist conceptions of the living body, and then argues:

> *"Thus, experience of one's own body runs counter to the reflective procedure which detaches subject and object from each other, and which gives us only the thought about the body, or the body as an idea, and not the experience of the body or the body as a reality. Descartes was well aware of this, since a famous letter of his to Elisabeth draws the distinction between the body as it is conceived through use in living and the body as it is conceived by intellect."*
> (Merleau-Ponty, 1945, 231/199)

When comprehending Merleau-Ponty's point of view, it is safe to say that the somatic marker theory proposed by Antonio Damasio is based on the same arguments and premises, when investigating why and how we use our feelings and past experiences to build ourselves and base our decision making, and also how our brains interact with our body to support such functions.

Reminding us that we are "bodies that think", Damasio argues that our feelings seem to be an unstoppable force. When we turn to emotions, we can find answers to explain human consciousness and cultures.

Sharing the same idea, Rainer Schandry and his colleagues focused their research on heartbeat perception and the related mental activity, which we have discussed in my book and which – I hope – makes you feel and think a bit deeply (in a positive way) moving forward.

Back when René Descartes proposed, *"Cogito, ergo sum,"* originally appearing in French, *"Je pense, donc je suis,"* he explained that we could not doubt our existence while in doubt. He further argued that the act of questioning one's own existence served as proof of the reality of one's mind.

In today's world, we have evidence to back the idea of our body and mind's intercorrelation as an interconnected unit. Our ability to make decisions, reason, judge, and learn is not only based on our mind's judgment. In fact, it is based on how our mind and body relate to past experiences in the physical world via our bodies; through gestures, sensations, feelings, and emotions. We have evidence that feelings of pain or pleasure or some quality in between are the bedrock of our body and mind.

Given the ubiquity of feelings, one would have thought that science would have elucidated long ago what feelings are, how they work, what they mean. But there are still so many questions about feelings.

What is a feeling? What are emotions?

Consider the experience of emotions, all the changes that an external observer can identify when you feel "happy" or "sad". Other changes cannot be identified by an external observer: For example, the heart beating faster. You perceive your own heartbeat internally.

However, all of these changes are being signalled continuously to the brain through the nerve terminals that bring to it impulses from skin, blood vessels, voluntary muscles, and so on. So, even though people cannot observe these changes, they are constantly happening inside of you—your feelings.

We can observe different emotions from an outside perspective. We can see when someone is sad or happy, and we can then try and figure out why someone is experiencing certain emotions. But feelings, which can be distinguished from emotions, were, and are still, some sort of mystery, and the core of them was inaccessible. We could not really get behind feelings.

When Antonio Damasio encountered the reality of neurological patients, their symptoms then forced him to investigate their conditions.

Imagine meeting someone who has a damage to a certain location of his brain and therefore became unable to feel compassion or embarrassment, yet still able to feel happy or sad.

Or imagine meeting someone who became unable to experience fear when fear was the appropriate reaction to the situation, because of damage located elsewhere in the brain; yet this person can still be compassionate.

It seemed clear that different brain systems controlled different feelings; damage to one area of the brain anatomy did not cause all types of feelings to disappear at once. Most surprisingly, when patients lost the ability to express a certain emotion, they also lost the ability to experience the corresponding feeling. But the opposite was not true: Some patients who lost their ability to experience certain feelings still could express the corresponding emotions.

Antonio Damasio also addressed the role of emotion and feeling in decision-making: the feeling of what happens outlined the role of emotion and feeling in the construction of the self. He states that feelings are the expression of human flourishing or human distress, as they occur in mind and body. Feelings are not a mere decoration added on to the emotions, something one might keep or discard. Feelings often are revelations of the state of life within the entire organism.

Most feelings are expressions of the struggle for balance, ideas of the exquisite adjustments and corrections without which, one mistake too many, the whole act collapses. Feelings can be revelatory of our simultaneous smallness and greatness.

How that revelation comes to mind is beginning to be revealed. The brain uses a number of dedicated brain regions working in concert to portray aspects of the body's activities in the form of neural maps. This portrait is a composite, an ever-changing picture of your life, or even yourself. The neural and chemical channels bring into the brain the signals with which this life portrait can be painted. The mystery of how we feel is a little less mysterious now.

Trying to understand the neurobiology of feelings and their antecedent emotions contributes to our views on the mind-body, which is something that is central to understanding who we are.

Emotion and related reactions are aligned with the body, feelings with the mind. The investigation of how thoughts trigger emotions and of how bodily emotions become the kind of thoughts we call feelings provides a privileged view into our minds and bodies. This, in return, creates the interwoven human organism.

Trying to understand what feelings are, how they work, and what they mean is indispensable to the future construction of a view of human beings. Especially when it comes to the core question of who we are.

Understanding our emotions and feelings is a key to the formulation of principles that are capable of reducing our distress and enhancing our flourishing. As humans, we deal with unresolved tensions of interpretations of our own existence. Understanding the human organism thus might help to get to the core of certain tensions and make them flourish. In other words, develop strength out of these tensions.

Our feelings and emotions give rise to somatic markers, which are guideposts that help steer our behaviour. Feelings are thus interconnected with our body-mind.

Thus, "We feel, therefore we are?"

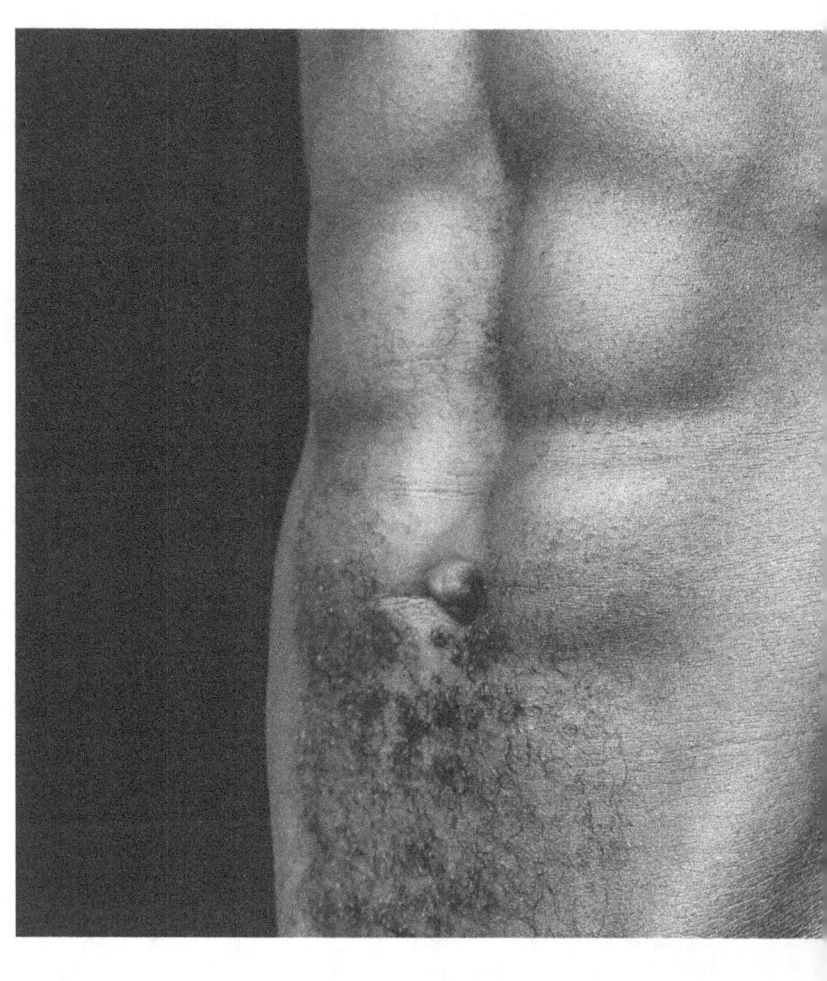

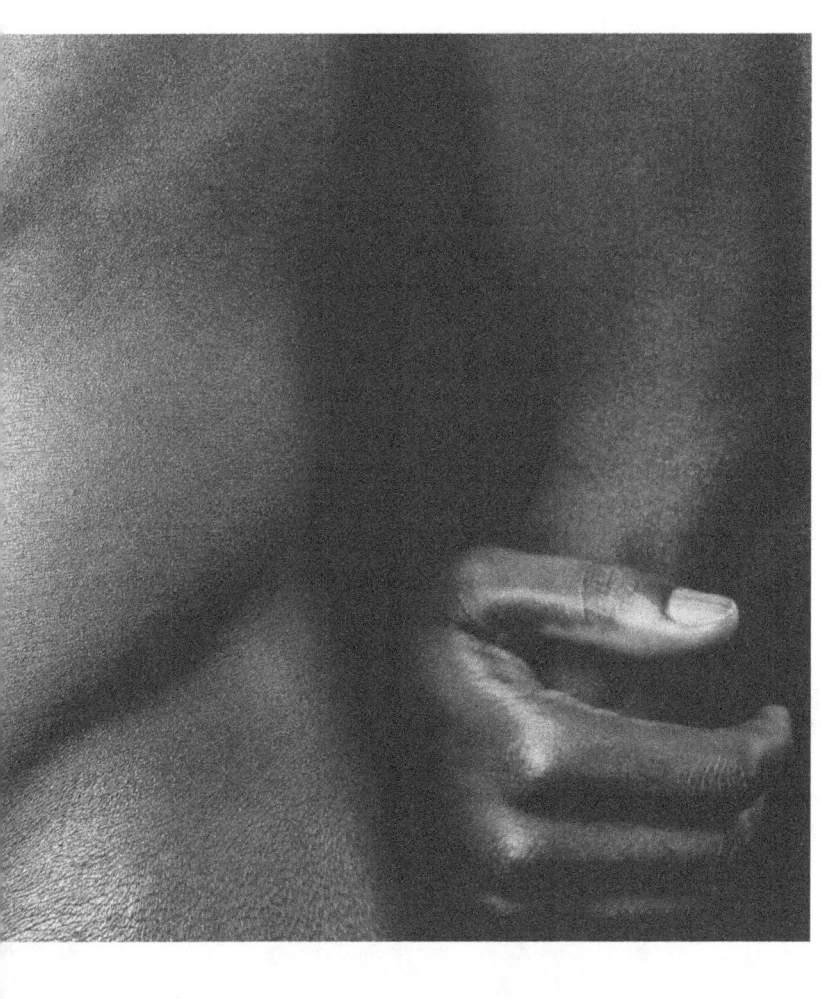

6. ENHANCING INNER AWARENESS THROUGH MINDFULNESS AND SELF-PERCEPTION

You read a book about the heart, the brain and the heart-brain, about how listening to our heartbeats may enhance our decision-making; you read a book about human identity. And while I will end this book by giving a new perspective on human identity, explaining why, from a scientific and philosophical perspective, it makes sense to look at the heart when questioning who we are, I would like to give you some tips on how you can enhance inner awareness.

Mindfulness and Self-Perception may be a bit common to you. Yet you might not really be aware of their potential and lack some sort of motivation to practice being mindful. Most of the time, this comes from a lack of knowing the Why.

What does mindfulness, meditation, music, and art do within us, mainly our bodies?

Amidst the demands and challenges of modern life, we've lost touch with the intuitive instincts of our body. All hope is not lost, however, because we can tune into ourselves once again through a process known as interoception. Cultural, technological, and medical developments mean that we've fallen out of touch with our internal self and have become poor interoceptors. When experiencing stress or anxiety, for example, we may seek solace in the escapism provided by drugs or alcohol. Throwing ourselves into our work or education might be a coping mechanism we use to distract ourselves from pressures within our personal relationships.

Regardless of the method, the reality is that seeking avoidance means we have lost our connection with our bodies. Interoception is defined as the level of awareness we have when it comes to feeling and interpreting the internal signals of our bodies, such as the rate of our heartbeat or sensations such as hunger and thirst. Through interoception, our mind makes sense of these signals and creates a map navigating our body's inner world, connecting it to our external experiences.

The level of perception enabled by interoception functions along the conscious and unconscious realm, and when this is disrupted, the implications for our emotional and psychological well-being are vast. Disrupted interoception is a component within most psychiatric disorders, and can exacerbate conditions, such as anxiety, mood disorders, and addiction.

The implication, therefore, is that learning methods of strengthening and fine-tuning interoception will lead to enhanced self-awareness, and resilience to developing mental disorders. Through understanding our internal state, we also heighten our awareness of those we interact with and their emotional state, and this elevated social understanding increases feelings of social rapport and community, which in turn boosts overall well-being. Interoception training could enable us to develop a more nuanced understanding of the self and our broader purpose.

The roots of interoception stretch much further in time than the beginnings of modern psychology, and traces are apparent in ancient traditions such as Indian and Chinese medicine. Within these timeless practices, interoception is represented as energy flowing throughout our body, bringing everything together into a cohesive system. Yoga, for example, strives to combine callisthenics with interoception and mindfulness. This knowledge can be enhanced by technology, with equipment now available that can provide us with first-hand insights into these internal body signals, thus creating innovative forms of biofeedback that perfect the art of self-awareness.

Within a contemporary context, technological developments have only increased the opportunities provided by the therapeutical application of interoception, particularly through digital platforms.

Awareness of the self has been regarded as the ultimate achievement of inner peace, emotional stability and mental clarity for millennia. With digital technology, we can differentiate true awareness from pure thought by integrating modern neuroscientific insights regarding the networks processing awareness with our actual subjective experiences of awareness. Our body is an incredibly intricate network, and true awareness is attained by understanding that the corporeal intelligence of our gut and heat is just as important as the cerebral intelligence of our brain, working in seamless unison.

Interoception intersects with mindfulness, because through learning to understand the internal signals of our body, we receive novel insights when it comes to the perceptions we have of ourselves as well as the environment surrounding us. As so exquisitely expressed by Joiner, the mindfulness adopted by modern society has become one of "superficiality, mediocrity and selfishness" – a mindfulness that encourages detachment and disembodiment. This encourages a shallow pursuit of everything that is material and temporary, rather than honouring thousands of years of evolutionary processes which have ensured that we have not only survived but flourished and prospered even in the face of immense difficulty.

Mindfulness can never be self-centred or selfish, and we are just beginning to realise, once again, that mindfulness is a holistic description of the universe and our role within it. True mindfulness is attained once we realise that our body is inextricably connected with our mind, soul, the people we interact with, and the wider universe surrounding us. At the heart of mindfulness is an awareness of the self so finely tuned that our conscious and unconscious mind and body function in perfect unison. The sense of grounded stability we feel within ourselves will be reflected in society. Mindfulness is like throwing a pebble into the ocean, the ripples of which will radiate outwards into the vast expanse of our collective conscience, and their reverberations will be felt so much further than the spaces we occupy.

Mindfulness Practises to Reduce Stress and Achieve Inner Peace

At the heart of mindfulness is developing an understanding of our unconscious and conscious selves to reach a heightened level of awareness and perception. Crucial to this is remembering that this can only be achieved by living in the present and appreciating even the smallest moments in life for their intrinsic meaning and purpose. Mindfulness is such a beautiful and comprehensive approach to life because it is so easy to implement, and for those who understand, mindfulness can be implemented into every one of our daily activities, duties, and routines. Some of the ways mindfulness can be incorporated into our lives include exercise, scented yoga, breathing, meditation, music, as well as art.

Mindful Exercise

Through mindful exercise, for example, we do not merely go through the motions of physically moving our body, but instead pay close attention to the processes and movements happening within us, whether that is the tension of our muscles, our fluctuating heartbeat, our breathing, or feelings of resistance. Mindfulness in exercise enables us to truly understand how exercise benefits the body and mind as a whole, enhancing our energy levels and the positive psychological and biological effects of exercise.

Scented Yoga

Integrating mindfulness with scented yoga is another incredibly intuitive and fulfilling experience. Yoga is an ancient tradition that is centred on aligning and concentrating the energies flowing throughout our bodies. When combined with aromatherapy, this creates an immersive and truly therapeutic experience. The ultimate aim of meditation techniques such as yoga is to achieve a state of pure awareness, and a scent such as a fragrant candle of an incense stick encourages a meditative and reflective state.

Breathing

Mindful breathing is one of the simplest, and yet most powerful, forms of mindfulness meditation. It is meant to inspire a deep meditative state, and through focusing on our breathing, we are at once perfecting and expressing our gratitude for one of the fundamental requirements of life. The intentions behind mindful breathing are to concentrate on the process of inhaling and exhaling, the natural rhythm and flow of breathing, and the way it feels within our lungs and upon our lips.

Meditation

Within the last few years, mindfulness meditation has been increasingly recognized as a powerful instrument for mental and emotional clarity. Essentially, it is a mental training practice during which you will focus on completing simple breathing practices and develop an awareness of your body and mind. The ultimate motivation for this approach is to release any feelings of negativity locked away inside, deescalate stress and perfect the intuition of your mind and body in order to achieve tranquillity and awareness.

Music

Music enhances the mindfulness experience, and it is a wonderful accompaniment to other practices such as meditation and breathing. By concentrating on the lyrics, rhythms, beat and instruments within a musical piece, you can learn a powerful lesson about being present in the moment, which is at the core of mindfulness practices. Through connecting with the music, you can hone your ability to focus and ignore all distractions, whilst simultaneously being exposed to an inspiring source of energy and creativity.

Art

In many ways, art is the ultimate form of creativity and expression, and this is why it can be applied so meaningfully to mindfulness practices. Art is made up of many components, such as colour, shapes, patterns, textures, light, and shadows, and each of them requires us to be entirely focused on living in the moment and making the most of every brushstroke, pencil-line and chalk-mark we make. Art doesn't require any training or experience, and by creating art with pure freedom, you can explore your natural curiosity and passion whilst expressing your emotions and feelings as you experience them.

Mindfulness is the art of being truly present in the moment and realising one's purpose and dreams through every action we take in our daily lives, no matter how mundane or seemingly insignificant. The intention is not to empty your mind, but rather to become so in touch with your thoughts and surroundings that every aspect of your life becomes a way to realize your purpose and unleash your true potential. Each of these mindfulness practices can be integrated with one another in order to create an immersive experience that is perfectly tailored to you. Breathing exercises, for example, could be supplemented with scented yoga and music, or combine mindful music with mindful art in order to tap into your creative potential and explore your thoughts and emotions.

7. LISTEN TO YOUR HEARTBEAT

Who are you? Who do you love? What do you love? How are our heartbeats related to our happiness?

While chasing happiness in life might be a quest and adventurous path in some way, the first step always starts on the inside. It is crucial to discover our true passion, what motivates us to keep moving forward in our human journey.

Finding the true meaning of being human and how we can evolve into a more meaningful existence in this world often comes across to happiness and love, more than just being, but also feeling.

Happiness is a choice, and so is love. Like the heart and the brain seem to be interconnected, listening to the heartbeats will give us many answers on what nourishes our aspirations in life, how we live our lives, how we fill the time with things that matter.

While paying close attention to the impulses and stimuli we receive in all lives, we identify what causes our vibration to change, making our hearts beat faster or stronger, which engages and excites us. While you are alive and while your heart beats, let it beat for people you love, for a profession you love and a life you love.

We are and always will be a work in progress, which is the beauty of being human. It is a fascinating human journey. Our existence is based on our journey in the material world and how we discover our conscious path to living a better and more meaningful life.

As long as our hearts are beating inside of us and our brains are working, then our body and soul will function in remarkable unison and perfect synchrony, looking forward to making the best decision for our lives.

We are in constant evolution, creating and redefining ourselves throughout our past experiences and actions. The heart-brain connection is a spring containing the waters of consciousness. If we learn to listen to this dialogue, we will see our reflection and truly understand ourselves with clarity and insight.

We are one.

The heart on the brain: Are heartbeats part of our identity?

Are we the beat of our hearts?

As our heart and brain work as one cohesive unit, we are all alike and yet unique in our own individualities. All based on our origins and individual experiences in life. If signals from the heart influence brain processes and the brain, it controls our thoughts in return. Maybe the heartbeats are a part of who we are.

At the very beginning, we might be predefined by our origins and consciously decide who we want to become and how we want to live. Thousands of other fractions give each of us an individual identity, and as unique individuals, we form a unity.

Continuing our journey to evolve into a better individual is a big part of being human.

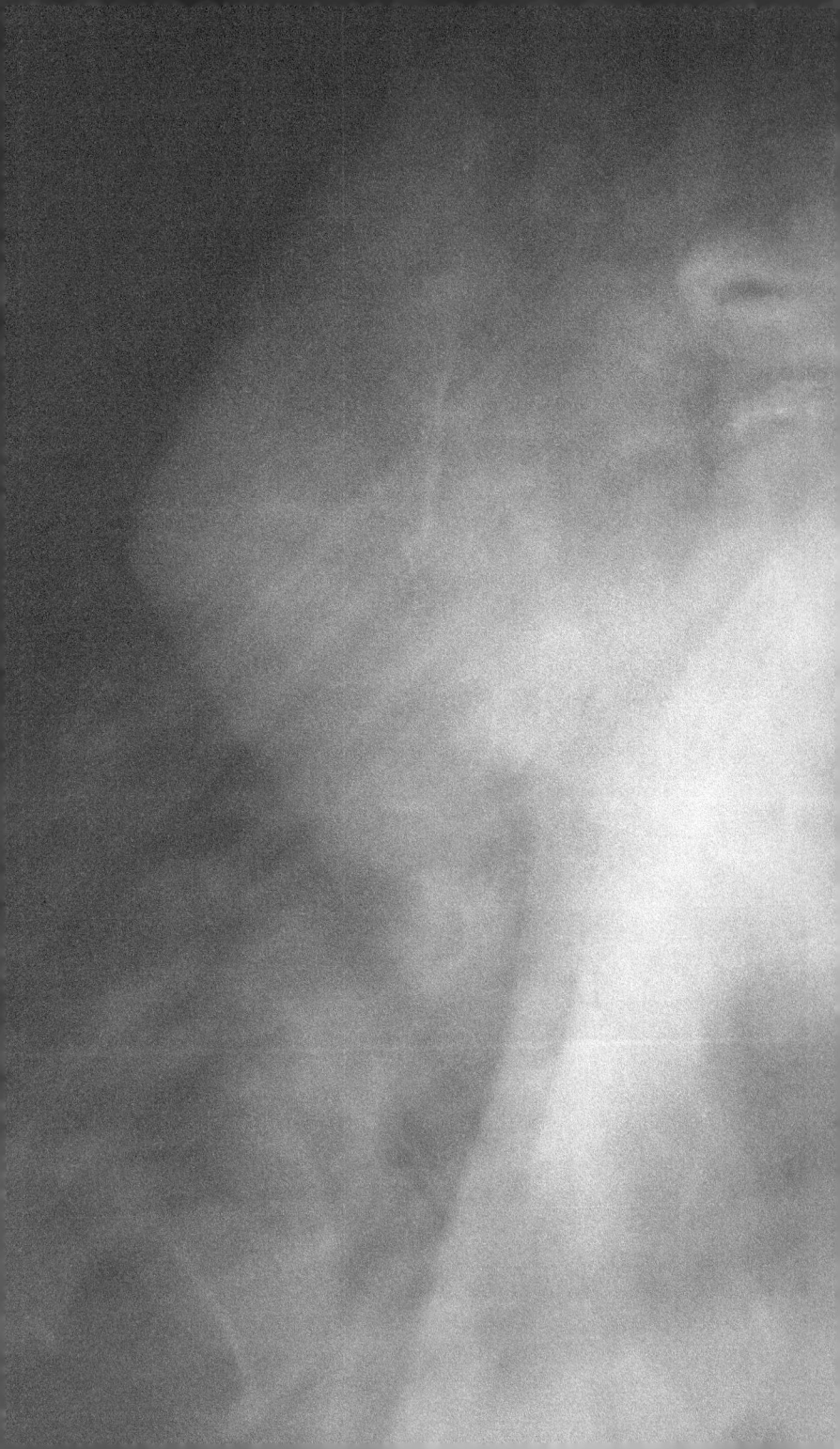

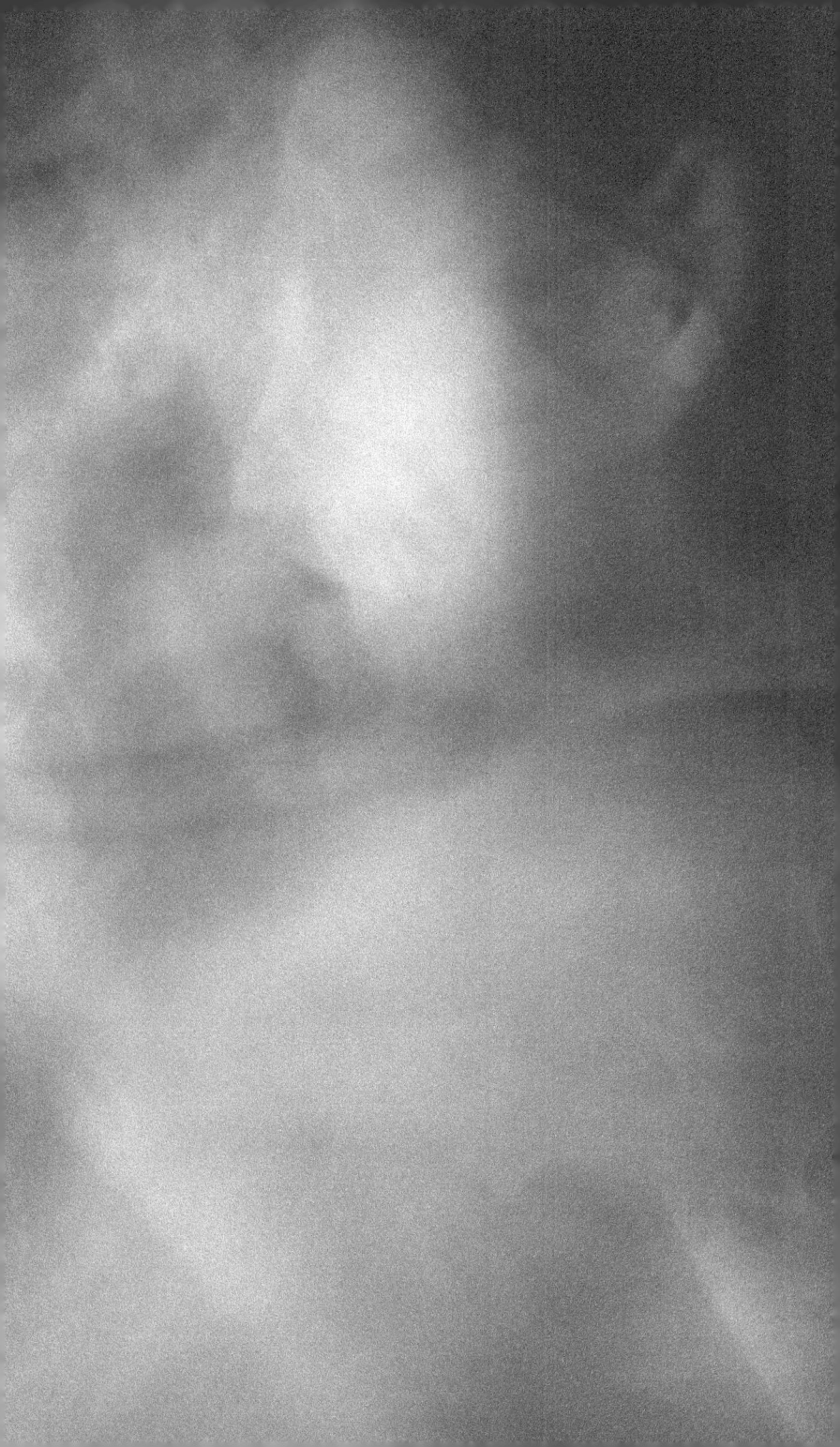

ACKNOWLEDGEMENTS

Photography by Manuela Sezer.

I would like to thank you, Manuela, for your incredible work. I am humbled and grateful for our friendship. My heart is smiling.

To everyone who contributed to the images, I cannot thank you enough for your great help. You are magnificent! A special thank you to Alain-Hervé Mfomkpa and Lisa Perissinotto!

Thank you, Oliver Look, for your artistic input, the *'Ikonenbilder'* and all your work inspires me and many others.

To my family: Thank you for your love and support. To my sisters, my parents, my grandparents, my cousins, and all other family members, thank you for always being there. To all the new family members, our next generation. To those who are already here with us and those who are going to join us in the future. To carrying children of my own. You are a blessing to me! Family is where our story begins.

I would like to thank my best friend for always being here for me during the good and the hard times and my closest friends for their inspiration and care for one another. A big thank you, with a lot of love.

Thank you to my coaches and team athletes. Sports made me. I am extremely thankful for everything that you do. Having coaches and team athletes that help and inspire me, made me realize what I need to improve as an athlete and as a person in general.

Warmest thank you to my academic mentors and colleagues for the opportunities, guidance, and support in my academic career. I truly appreciate my supervisors and all the help, thoughtfulness, and talks with my colleagues during coffee breaks. Thank you to everyone who helps me in research and education. It means so much to me.

I would like to thank novum, the author support, the team, and the book reviewers. You are always so helpful.

Thank you from the bottom of my heart.

ENDNOTES

Antoni, H. (1989). Function of the Heart. In Schmidt, Robert F., Thews, Gerhard (Eds.) *Human Physiology* (2nd ed., pp. 439–479). Springer.

Aziz, Q., Thompson, D. G., Ng, V. W. K., Hamdy, S., Sarkar, S., Brammer, M. J., ... & Williams, S. C. R. (2000). Cortical processing of human somatic and visceral sensation. Journal of Neuroscience, 20(7), 2657–2663.

Basar, E. (1999). Brain function and oscillations. II. Integrative brain function. Neurophysiology and cognitive processes.

Bechara, A., Tranel, D., & Damasio, H. (2000). Characterization of the decision-making deficit of patients with ventromedial prefrontal cortex lesions. Brain, 123(11), 2189–2202.

Bechara, A., Damasio, H., & Damasio, A. (2000). Emotion, decision making and the orbitofrontal cortex. Cerebral Cortex (New York, N.Y. 1991), 10(3), 295–307.

Brener, J. (1977). Visceral perception. In *Biofeedback and Behavior* (pp. 235–259). Springer, Boston, MA.

Brener, J., & Jones, J. M. (1974). Interoceptive discrimination in intact humans: Detection of cardiac activity. Physiology & Behavior, 13(6), 763–767.

Cameron, O. G. (2001). Interoception: the inside story—a model for psychosomatic processes. Psychosomatic medicine, 63(5), 697–710.

Changbo Lu Tao Yang Huan Zhao Ming Zhang Fancheng Meng Hao Fu Yingli Xie Hui Xu. (2016). Insular Cortex is Critical for the Perception, Modulation,and Chronification of Pain. Neuroscience Bulletin, 32(2), 191–201.

Damasio, A. R., Tranel, D., & Damasio, H. C. (1991). Somatic markers and the guidance of behavior: Theory and preliminary testing. In H. S. Levin, H. M. Eisenberg, & A. L. Benton (Eds.), Frontal lobe function and dysfunction (p. 217–229). Oxford University Press.

Damasio, A. R. (1994). Descartes' error: Emotion, rationality and the human brain.

Damasio, A. R. (1994). Descartes' error and the future of human life. Scientific American, 271(4), 144-144.

Damasio, A., & Damasio, H. (1996). Neurobiology of Decision-Making (1st ed. 1996.). Springer Berlin Heidelberg.

Damasio, A. R. (2000). The feeling of what happens: Body and emotion in the making of consciousness. Houghton Mifflin Harcourt.

Damasio, A. R. (2003). Looking for Spinoza: Joy, sorrow, and the feeling brain. Houghton Mifflin Harcourt.

Ehlers, A., Margraf, J., Roth, W., Taylor, C., & Birbaumer, N. (1988). Anxiety induced by false heart rate feedback in patients with panic disorder. Behaviour Research and Therapy, 26(1), 1–11.

Ehlers, A., Mayou, R. A., Sprigings, D. C., & Birkhead, J. (2000). Psychological and perceptual factors associated with arrhythmias and benign palpitations. Psychosomatic Medicine, 62(5), 693–702.

Ferguson, M. L., & Katkin, E. S. (1996). Visceral perception, anhedonia, and emotion. Biological Psychology, 42(1–2), 131–145.

Hanamori, T., Kunitake, T., Kato, K., & Kannan, H. (1998). Neurons in the posterior insular cortex are responsive to gustatory stimulation of the pharyngolarynx, baroreceptor and chemoreceptor stimulation, and tail pinch in rats. Brain Research, 785(1), 97–106.

Herbert, B. M., Herbert, C., & Pollatos, O. (2011). On the relationship between interoceptive awareness and alexithymia: is interoceptive awareness related to emotional awareness? Journal of personality, 79(5), 1149–1175.

Jones, G. E. (1994). Perception of visceral sensations: A review of recent findings, methodologies, and future directions. In P. Ackles, J.R. Jennings, and M.G.H. Coles (Eds.) *Advances in Psychophysiology* (Vol. 5, pp. 55–192). Jessica Kingsley Publishers.

Jones, G. E., Leonberger, T. F., Rouse, C. H., Caldwell, J. A., & Jones, K. R. (1986). Preliminary data exploring the presence of an evoked potential associated with cardiac visceral activity. Psychophysiology, 23(445).

Katkin, E. S., Wiens, S., & Öhman, A. (2001). Nonconscious fear conditioning, visceral perception, and the development of gut feelings. Psychological Science, 12(5), 366–370.

Klimesch, W., Schack, B., & Sauseng, P. (2005). The functional significance of theta and upper alpha oscillations. Experimental psychology, 52(2), 99–108.

Leopold, C., & Schandry, R. (2001). The heartbeat-evoked brain potential in patients suffering from diabetic neuropathy and in healthy control persons. Clinical Neurophysiology, 112(4), 674–682.

Libet B, Gleason CA, Wright EW, Pearl DK. Time of conscious intention to act in relation to onset of cerebral activity (readiness-potential). The unconscious initiation of a freely voluntary act. Brain. 1983 Sep;106 (Pt 3):623–42. doi: 10.1093/brain/106.3.623. PMID: 6640273.

Libet, B. (2002). The timing of mental events: Libet's experimental findings and their implications.

Martínez-Selva JM, Sánchez-Navarro JP, Bechara A, Román F. Mecanismos cerebrales de la toma de decisiones [Brain mechanisms involved in decision-making]. Rev Neurol. 2006 Apr 1-15;42(7):411–8. Spanish. PMID: 16602058.

Merleau-Ponty, M. (1945). Phénoménologie de la perception, Gallimard. Paris: Bibliothèque des idées.

Merleau-Ponty, M. (1964). L'Œil et l'esprit. Paris: Gallimard.

Montoya, P., Schandry, R., & Müller, A. (1993). Heartbeat evoked potentials (HEP): Topography and influence of cardiac awareness and focus of attention. Electroencephalography and Clinical Neurophysiology/Evoked Potentials Section, 88(3), 163–172.

Mussgay, L., Klinkenberg, N., & Ruddel, H. (1999). Heart beat perception in patients with depressive, somatoform, and personality disorders. Journal of Psychophysiology, 13(1), 27–36.

Nagai, M., Hoshide, S., & Kario, K. (2010). The insular cortex and cardiovascular system: A new insight into the brain-heart axis. Journal of the American Society of Hypertension, 4(4), 174–182.

Nieuwenhuys, R., Voogd, J., & van Huijzen, C. (1988). Human Central Nervous System: A Synopsis and Atlas (Third Revised Edition.). Springer Berlin/Heidelberg.

Pollatos, O., & Schandry, R. (2004). Accuracy of heartbeat perception is reflected in the amplitude of the heartbeat-evoked brain potential. Psychophysiology, 41(3), 476–482.

Pollatos, O., & Schandry, R. (2008). Emotional processing and emotional memory are modulated by interoceptive awareness. Cognition & Emotion, 22(2), 272–287.

Pollatos, O., Gramann, K., & Schandry, R. (2007). Neural systems connecting interoceptive awareness and feelings. Human brain mapping, 28(1), 9–18.

Pollatos, O., Herbert, B. M., Matthias, E., & Schandry, R. (2007). Heart rate response after emotional picture presentation is modulated by interoceptive awareness. International Journal of Psychophysiology, 63(1), 117–124.

Pollatos, O., Traut-Mattausch, E., Schroeder, H., & Schandry, R. (2007). Interoceptive awareness mediates the relationship between anxiety and the intensity of unpleasant feelings. Journal of anxiety disorders, 21(7), 931–943.

Riordan, H., Squires, N. K., & Brener, J. (1990). Cardio-cortical potentials: Electrophysiological evidence lot visceral perception. Psychophysiology, 27(S59).

Sidebotham, D., & Le Grice, I. J. (2007). Physiology and pathophysiology. In Cardiothoracic Critical Care (p. 9). Butterworth-Heinemann Elsevier, Philadelphia, PA.

Sidebotham, D. (2007). Cardiothoracic critical care. Elsevier Health Sciences.

Shaffer, F., & Ginsberg, J. P. (2017). An Overview of Heart Rate Variability Metrics and Norms. *Frontiers in Public Health*, 5, 258.

Schandry, R. (1981). Heartbeat perception and emotional experience. Psychophysiology, 18(4), 483–488.

Schandry, R., & Montoya, P. (1996). Event-related brain potentials and the processing of cardiac activity. Biological Psychology, 42(1), 75–85.

Schandry, R., Sparrer, B., & Weitkunat, R. (1986). From the heart to the brain: A study of heartbeat contingent scalp potentials, International Journal of Neuroscience, 30(4), 261–275.

Waxenbaum, J. A., Reddy, V., & Varacallo, M. (2020). Anatomy, Autonomic Nervous System. In StatPearls. StatPearls Publishing.

Werner, N. S., Jung, K., Duschek, S., & Schandry, R. (2009). Enhanced cardiac perception is associated with benefits in decision-making. Psychophysiology, 46(6), 1123–1129.

Graphics from Shutterstock.

The author

Cléa Formaz is a Swiss researcher and PhD candidate at ETH Zürich and holds a Master of Science degree in Cognitive Neuroscience. She developed an interest in heart-brain interaction as a teenager, when she started testing her physical and mental limits in athletics. This interest was further piqued by studying undergraduate psychology and ruminating on the meaning of humanity. Formaz also enjoys art, literature, and athletics, specifically middle distance running. This is her first book.

www.ingramcontent.com/pod-product-compliance
Lightning Source LLC
Chambersburg PA
CBHW070039180226
39896CB00003B/183